# FORGING PATHWAYS TO IMPROVISE MUSIC

A step-by-step resource on forging one's own pathway to improvise music, this book guides the musician through a clear and simple method that will easily translate to the reader's genre of choice.

Many musicians struggle with improvisation. Coincidentally, educators also find it challenging to integrate improvisation into curriculum. This book breaks down the barriers most performers and educators combat in the learning and teaching of improvisation, and is a helpful approach to demystify the complicated sphere of music improvisation. Divided into three sections, the first part of the book helps the reader develop an improvisatorial mindset to mentally conceive musical ideas, regardless of genre. The second portion then connects the improviser's mindset to translating those ideas into a compelling musical performance in real time. The book's final third assists the reader with discovering how to apply this method of improvisation to the nuanced liturgical, comedic, jazz, and classical styles.

*Forging Pathways to Improvise Music* offers a practical introduction to improvisational methods essential for educators, students, and musicians of diverse educational backgrounds and musical genres.

**Joseph Montelione** has worked with Billy Joel, Tony Bennett, Patti LaBelle, Charlie Daniels, Amy Grant, Steven Curtis Chapman, The Irish Tenors, Ruben Studdard, Mandisa, Kim Choo-ja, The Little River Band, Julie Andrews, Nathan Lane, Lou Diamond Phillips, Ian Fraser, Laura Bell Bundy, Frankie Valli, Michael Bublé, and many others. He is a member of the Walt Disney World Orchestra, with affiliations with Sarasota Orchestra, Florida Orchestra, Orlando Philharmonic, Opera Tampa, Jacksonville Symphony, Coastal Symphony of Georgia, Opera Memphis, Memphis Symphony, Alabama Symphony, Moscow State Radio Symphony, Bayreuth Festival Orchestra, Washington Symphony Orchestra, to name a few. He has been seen on Broadway with shows such as *A Funny Thing Happened on the Way to the Forum*, *Victor/Victoria*, *The King and I*, and *Big: The Musical*, as well as first national tours such as *Wicked* and Disney's *Aladdin*. As a music director, Montelione has conducted a variety of groups including the Memphis Chamber Players, New Ballet Ensemble, West Point Military Academy Band, the Capistrano Performing Arts Center Orchestra, and Norwegian Cruise Lines. Additionally, he has held teaching positions at the University of Florida, Rhodes College, Florida Tech University, and the Los Angeles Philharmonic. More information is available at www.montemusicservices.com.

# Forging Pathways to Improvise Music
For Classical, Jazz, Comedic, and Church Musicians

**Joseph Montelione**

NEW YORK AND LONDON

Designed cover image: Chamopcs, Shutterstock

First published 2024
by Routledge
4 Park Square, Milton Park, Abingdon, Oxon OX14 4RN

and by Routledge
605 Third Avenue, New York, NY 10158

*Routledge is an imprint of the Taylor & Francis Group, an informa business*

© 2024 Joseph Montelione

The right of Joseph Montelione to be identified as author of this work has been asserted in accordance with sections 77 and 78 of the Copyright, Designs and Patents Act 1988.

All rights reserved. No part of this book may be reprinted or reproduced or utilised in any form or by any electronic, mechanical, or other means, now known or hereafter invented, including photocopying and recording, or in any information storage or retrieval system, without permission in writing from the publishers.

*Trademark notice*: Product or corporate names may be trademarks or registered trademarks, and are used only for identification and explanation without intent to infringe.

*British Library Cataloguing-in-Publication Data*
A catalogue record for this book is available from the British Library

*Library of Congress Cataloging-in-Publication Data*
Names: Montelione, Joseph, author.
Title: Forging pathways to improvise music : for classical, jazz, comedic, and church
    musicians / Joseph Montelione.
Identifiers: LCCN 2023011598 (print) | LCCN 2023011599 (ebook) | ISBN 9781032377742
    (hardback) | ISBN 9781032377735 (paperback) | ISBN 9781003341857 (ebook)
Subjects: LCSH: Improvisation (Music) | Music—Instruction and study.
Classification: LCC MT68 .M595 2023 (print) | LCC MT68 (ebook) | DDC 781.3/6—dc23/
    eng/20230310
LC record available at https://lccn.loc.gov/2023011598
LC ebook record available at https://lccn.loc.gov/2023011599

ISBN: 9781032377742 (hbk)
ISBN: 9781032377735 (pbk)
ISBN: 9781003341857 (ebk)

DOI: 10.4324/9781003341857

Typeset in Times New Roman
by Apex CoVantage, LLC

# Contents

| | |
|---|---|
| *Preface* | *viii* |
| *Introduction* | *xi* |

## Chapter 1 – The Essential Elements     1

*Ten skills needed to create an improviser's mindset  1*
*Why Improvise? – The Ten Effects of Improvisation  5*

## Chapter 2 – Hear What To Play: An Introduction to Intention     10

*Mentally Conceive an Idea—The Intention  11*
*Awareness Exercises  12*
*Music Intention Exercises  13*

## Chapter 3 – Establish an Improvisational Mindset     22

*Imagination Etudes  22*
*Group Mind Exercises  26*

## Chapter 4 – Play What You Hear: An Introduction to Invention     37

*Musical Conversation Exercises  37*
*Translate the Idea into a Musical Reality—The Invention  38*
*Improviser as Part Composer, Part Performer, and Part Listener  42*

## Chapter 5 – Embroider a Solo: Improvise Between Notes     44

*Different Types of Musical Enhancements – What To Play  44*
*Embroider Exercises to Aid in Applying Choices  50*
*Essential Elements Applied When Embroidering the Original Line  54*

## Chapter 6 – Construct a Solo: Compose in Real Time     57

*Explore Melody  57*
*Discover Harmony  59*
*Understanding the Form  64*
*Internalize the Nuances  65*

vi   *Contents*

*Know that Imagination Is Limited to What Technique Allows  65*
*Essential Elements Applied When Constructing a Solo  66*

## Chapter 7 – Cultivate Creativity : Improvise Compelling Notes  69

*Inventiveness  70*
*Groove  72*
*Aesthetic Exercises  74*
*In a Creative Slump?  76*
*Essential Elements Applied When Constructing Creative Phrases  77*

## Chapter 8 – Understanding Jazz Language  81

*Improvisation for the Jazz Soloist: The signs and symbols of the language of jazz*
  *improvisation  82*
*The ii-V-I Progression  84*
*Pentatonic, Blues and the Seven/Three Resolution  85*
*The Secret Hidden Harmonic Code  89*
*Essential Elements Applied When Learning Jazz Language  92*

## Chapter 9 – Crossing Over: Jazz Improvisation for the Classical Musician  95

*Beginning to Cross Over  95*
*Got Style?  100*
*Transcribing the Experts  101*
*Avoiding Roadblocks  102*
*Essential Elements Applied When Crossing Over  106*

## Chapter 10 – Classical Language for the Jazz Improviser  110

*Medieval Music  110*
*Renaissance Music  111*
*Baroque Music  112*
*Cadenza, Prologue, Free and Chance Music  112*
*Essential Elements Applied When Learning Classical Language  114*

## Chapter 11 – Improvisation Exercises Inspired by Classical Genres  117

*Medieval-esque Music Exercises  117*
*Renaissance-like Music Exercises  119*
*Baroque-ish Music Exercises  126*
*Cadenza, Prologue, Free and Chance Music Exercises  136*
*Essential Elements Applied to Western Classical Improvisation  141*

## Chapter 12 – Understanding Improv Comedy Language  145

*Long Form Improv Comedy—What It Is and How It Incorporates Live Music  145*
*Do We Need Musical Accompaniment in This Form? If So, What For?  145*
*What is a Musical Improviser?  146*

*How a Musical Improviser Makes Up a Song  148*
*The Construction of an Improv Comedic Song  149*

## Chapter 13 – Improvisation for the Improv Comedic Musician

150

*How an Improv Comic Actor Makes Up Lyrics to a Song  150*
*Improvising Lyrics Exercises  150*
*Strategies to Improvise Songs  153*
*Things to Consider When Acting as a Musical Improviser  156*

## Chapter 14 – Liturgical Improvisation: Traditional and Contemporary

158

*The Dissection of Liturgical Music  158*
*Liturgical Improvisation Strategies  160*
*Timing Improvised Music to the Liturgy  166*
*Contemporary Christian Music: Reading a Lead Sheet  168*

*Final Thoughts*                175
*Bibliography*                  177
*Index*                         178

# Preface

The first time I improvised anything other than jazz was when a local church asked me to perform during a service. At a certain point in the service, I was instructed to play the refrain of a standard hymn. Then, on the last iteration, I was asked to play a descant. At the time, I was in high school and was not clear on what a descant was, plus there were no indications of a descant on the sheet music. Since this was a paying job and I still considered myself green, I was too intimidated to ask what a descant was. Just before the final iteration, I decided that a descant must be something different than the melody, so I improvised one and kept playing until the hymn was over. As the organist looked at me, I thought, *Here it is, this is where my career starts and ends. This is the moment where I pack up my horn and never leave my house again.* The organist said, "That wasn't the written descant for that hymn." I was thinking, *I know. I'm sorry, but if I knew what a descant was, I'd play it.* The organist continued, "That was better than the written descant. Good job!"

How was I able to do that? Was it something unique that only musicians with jazz improvisation experience could accomplish? Was I "talented"? Did I have an uncanny ability to improvise at a young age? No. It was a learned skill set like any other musical skill. So how can you learn to improvise? With regard to learning improvisation, Clark Terry said "*Imitate. Assimilate. Innovate.*" Or IAI. To broadly summarize this concept, a learner would listen to a master improviser, ingrain the nuances, and use what was learned in new and innovative ways. For some young musicians, the entry point to learn improvisation is not what is in this book; it's what's on the masters' recordings. So, how do you know if this is the right book for you?

IAI is an effective system of learning improvisation. After years of intensive study, learners memorize what they have heard in the past and use that as a source to help create their own improvisation. However, there are different types of learners. For learners who have limited or no experience playing by ear, IAI can seem overwhelming. These types of learners could view the plethora of music, harmonic devices, melodic lines, rhythmic interpretations, and other artistic nuances to absorb, as daunting tasks.

Learning to improvise a specific genre at the highest level involves listening to, memorizing, and internalizing a tremendous amount of music. It takes many years to master and a substantial amount of hard work. There's just no getting around that! To be clear, this book does not seek to circumvent the crucial steps of IAI. Rather, it seeks to introduce concepts of improvisation to would-be musicians in an approachable way. It is for those who may need a prerequisite course in understanding how to create something from nothing. This prerequisite course should better enable novice improvisers to be more receptive of approaches such as IAI. This book offers a different perspective on how to learn to develop an improvisational mindset.

While elements of IAI are mentioned throughout this book, it does not explicitly focus on the IAI learning process. There is little discussion on listening to or imitating improvisatory masters, nor much pedagogy to emphasize how improvisers assimilate repertoire and develop their own musical personality. There will be minimal references to composed or transcribed pieces of music and how one might learn them and use them as models—there are plenty of other books published on these subjects.

Now that we know what this book is not, let's address what the book is about! For the emerging market of learners who are not as skilled or developed with "playing" or "learning" by ear, this book breaks down the process of improvisation and offers alternatives to aid the learning process.

Improvisation can seem overwhelming and intimidating in the beginning. Throughout many years in the classroom, I have observed that novice improvisers struggle with two concepts: (1) activating an improvisational mindset (the "how") and (2) knowing the necessary notes to play in the moment (the "what"). To combat this, many educators introduce students to visual chord/scale relationships and written theory in the first lesson. This isn't an inherently poor tactic to learn improvisation, but it does not lend itself to help the student "learn by ear." Conversely, other educators may introduce the "Imitate, Assimilate, Innovate" methodology. As stated earlier, this particular method is an invaluable approach but could be overwhelming to beginners, especially those who have limited to no experience playing by ear. *What if there were a learning process that acts as a precursor to common teaching methods such as the IAI method? Is there another way to introduce improvisation in a digestible way without overwhelming a learner?* This book explores *how* (or what I call intention) to activate the improvisation process, followed by examining *what* (or what I call invention) could be played in the moment. The book also introduces how the relationship between the *how* and the *what* can apply to various genres.

Perhaps the improvisation learning process could look like this:

You will be introduced to strategies to help develop skill sets needed to begin your own journey in the path towards improvisational artistry. Think of this book as a foundational support system to prepare you for the study of more advanced techniques, such as imitating master improvisers, assimilating genre-specific repertoire, and developing their own musical personality. I hope that this book helps you develop an improvisational disposition that will prepare you to engage in your favorite musical genre.

I had the following types of musicians in mind during the writing process: music educators that teach at the high school and collegiate level, university music majors looking to jump-start core improvisation training, the professional musician with little to no exposure to improv, and active community musicians looking for avenues to include improvisation into their musical lives. This book is designed to help readers transform their practice and, ultimately, their performance. But how?

x  *Preface*

**To the Teacher**

Are you someone who teaches at a school that 1) trends toward a delineation between jazz studies and improvisation, 2) would like to add more improv courses for non-jazz students, or 3) offers non-genre improvisational ensembles, 4) needs a book that is accessible, easy to follow, and can work within a semester or two's course curriculum? Or perhaps you are a middle school or high school educator who finds it increasingly difficult to implement National Core Standard 3 (improvisation) into the classroom either because 1) you yourself find improvisation difficult or 2) there aren't any resources outside of elementary school that can appeal to middle and high school students? Then this book will help fill the void.

This book is structured in three sequential sections—intention, invention, and application. The first part of the book explores the benefits of improvisation and *how* to develop an improvisatorial mindset, regardless of genre. The second part will help connect the improviser's mindset to *what* could be played in the moment—acknowledging that both the *how* and the *what* skill sets are critical to successfully improvise. The book's final section is more application-oriented, where nuances of various musical styles, including jazz, classical, liturgical, and comedic traditions, present themselves.

Each of the 14 chapters intentionally gathers momentum, layering guidance and support by breaking tiered tasks into simple, more accessible applications—not only for the music instructor but for the musician as well. The sequential nature makes it ideal for a quick read, or it can take the professional or preprofessional musician on a structured semester or year's course of study, building from the origin of an idea to improvising a compelling solo. I encourage you to start with Chapter 1 and consecutively work your way through the book, rather than skipping around chapters.

**To the Student**

Are you someone who has a moderate level of technical facility on your instrument, basic musicianship skills, and music theory knowledge? Are you also someone who has no experience, or little experience with improvisation and is looking to learn, develop, and improve? When attempting to improvise jazz, do you experience roadblocks such as not knowing what to play, getting lost in the chord changes, connecting one chord to the next? Perhaps you are a budding church musician looking to get started but unsure of where to begin or a classical musician looking to begin to understand how to embellish a melody. Then this is the book for you.

If you are a student who needs to imitate, assimilate, and innovate, then do it. But if you are a student that needs a prerequisite course to Clark Terry's strategy to learning improv, then you need intention, invention, and application. It has been my experience that developing improv skills in a nonthreatening group can facilitate collaboration. Much like when you learn a new language, having a conversation with a native speaker will help develop your language skills. But if you are in the early stages of learning a language, you may not be able to contribute much to a conversation, and therefore need a bit more time to work out fundamentals. This book does not solely focus on one particular genre. It will introduce to you a process to improv that will forge pathways to multiple genres. It will help you develop an improvisational mind, exploring exercises and concepts to introduce you to processes to create and perform simultaneously.

# Introduction

Have you ever seen *The Music Man*? It's a musical about a traveling salesman who cons a small town into buying band instruments. Without giving away any spoilers, the main character, Harold Hill, talks about the think system. In the musical, his think system is based on all the band students needing to just think about the music, and they'll eventually be able to play it without having a significant amount of time developing the necessary technical skills to play an instrument. When it comes to learning improvisation, you need to put in the time to develop a certain level of fluency on your instrument to be able to showcase your understanding of music theory and basic musicianship. There are, however, other skill sets that need to be developed: intention, invention, and application. Intention, or the mental process that precede the playing of a note, can be a challenge to teach and learn, and is sometimes overlooked in improvisation pedagogy. This mental process, unlike the Harold Hill's fictional method, relies on a certain technical fluency on your instrument, and basic musicianship skills.

When I was a novice, I often got lost in changes as simple as a twelve-bar blues progression. At times, I drew blanks on what to play or, conversely, played too many notes. It was difficult for me to hear the harmony, and I would often struggle through complicated chord changes. I had a fluency on my instrument but still struggled with the spontaneous creation of notes in a performance. Ultimately, I discovered that the problem came down to my inability to tap into an improvisatorial mindset. I wrote this book to offer a different perspective on how to learn to develop this type of mindset and to help you navigate through the various tribulations that crowd the landscape of learning how to improvise.

The book opens with the benefits of improvisation. It advocates for the continued inclusion of improvisation as a core standard by examining the benefits and effects of studying improvisation throughout one's life. The book also presents exercises to help give teachers the confidence to implement National Content Standard 3 into their curriculum. The ten essential elements for the intention process are introduced and will help you better understand the core characteristics my experience has shown that every improviser must possess, regardless of level of technical mastery of the instrument. I return to the ten essential elements at the conclusion of the ensuing chapters.

The next chapter is an introduction to what I have called the *intention*, or the mental conception of an idea where you will discover ways to develop music intention. In chapter three, the goal is to create a sense of *how* to improvise by providing various exercises for soloists and chamber ensembles to help introduce or improve their basic improvisational skills, regardless of genre. The activities in this chapter will help bring out an improvisatory nature in a musician who primarily experiences music through reading pre-composed, printed music.

xii *Introduction*

What follows is an introduction to translating an idea in real time, which I refer to as the *invention* (or the *what*). Once there is a heightened sense of *how* to improvise, Chapter 5 helps you begin learning *what* to play. Chapter 6 answers the questions: *What do musicians need to create a solo? How do they start the process of creating an original one?* Chapter 7 includes a procedure to understand phrases related to groove and aesthetics. There are several aesthetic exercises to bring out the creative side of a solo, along with helpful ideas for climbing out of creative slumps.

As musicians build a stronger improvisatorial foundation through a series of layered exercises, they can begin to construct a more coherent, compelling solo that will eventually become more applicable to a specific genre. For Chapters 8 and 9, the marriage of intention and invention is applied to the language of jazz, and is then applied to the language of early Western European music before 1850 within Chapters 10 and 11. In Chapters 12 and 13, the intention to invention process is applied to improvised music within long-form improv comedy. Finally, in Chapter 14, the process is applied to traditional liturgical music and contemporary worship music.

So, what is the payoff for taking the time to read this book and apply the concepts? This book will help you to (1) have a better understanding of *how* to improvise, so an improvisatorial mindset develops, (2) take that understanding and connect it to *what* could be played in real time, and (3) be better prepared for a more focused study of your favorite musical genre.

# 1 The Essential Elements

What fundamental aspects of improvisation competence do musicians need to have in order to develop their improvisational mindset? The answer lies in their ability to manifest an extemporaneous blend of the following items: increased levels of trust, amplified listening skills, openness to collaboration, the ability to switch between large- and small-scale managerial thought processes, a heightened degree of awareness, receptiveness to new ideas, steadfast confidence, persistence in ongoing study sessions, intensified physical practice, and an active imagination. I believe these are the essential elements trained musicians must develop to maneuver through the world of improvisation. Improvisation can be daunting to someone who has not had much exposure, but with a strong work ethic, determination, dedication, an open mind, the following essential elements, and a concrete practice plan, any working or developing musician can achieve a positive outcome.

---

**Ten Essential Elements that Experienced Improvisers Exhibit**

1. Trust
2. Ability to listen
3. Synergy
4. Micromanagement and macromanagement
5. Realization
6. Stepping into the deep
7. Confidence
8. Genuine study of craft
9. Practice
10. Imagination

---

These ten essential elements will return at the conclusion of each of the ensuing chapters. Are there only ten elements needed to improvise successfully? No, these elements should not be viewed as the only skills necessary for improvisation. Think of them as key characteristics a musician should develop to foster an improviser's mind. I would encourage you to read the following chapters with the essential elements in mind. Then move on to see how they apply through this book's invention and subsequent application sections. Let us begin, though, by examining each of the ten elements.

DOI:10.4324/9781003341857-1

## 1. Trust

Whenever I improvise, I exhibit a high level of trust—either in myself or of others—in order for peak performance to occur in real time. Years of practicing the art of "letting go" create high levels of trust within oneself and with other musicians. I let go of all the superego tendencies the psyche may contain—essentially the inner critic. I think of the superego as a type of conscience that punishes misbehavior with feelings of guilt. Good improvisers become great improvisers when they 1) trust that they have infinite ideas in their mind's ear, and 2) these ideas will present themselves in the needed moment instead of preparing specific licks beforehand. Basically, they put more trust in creating in the moment than in anything a preset plan could potentially create. Trusting in the infinite Rolodex of information at a person's disposal, tapping into that bank of ideas, and making a withdrawal in the moment is paramount to experiencing the most accurate form of improvisation.

## 2. Ability to Listen

One of the key skills a successful improviser must master is the ability to listen to both the inner voice (not to be confused with the inner critic, as the inner voice is not critical and accepts all ideas without judgment) and the sounds coming from other improvisers. Listeners (in whatever form) in the context of music are to listen intently and react to their surroundings. The listener's role while performing improvisation is the same. As an experienced listener, I will be present in the moment, focusing on what the other person is creating, for example, harmonic voicings, rhythmic patterns, stylistic nuances, etc. I am empathetic and accept the other person's ideas, working together to form one cohesive sound. I am patient and allow other musicians a voice in the creative process. Whether you have the ability to assimilate large amounts of musical vocabulary or you are still in the beginning stages of learning to improvise, never stop actively listening to music. Listening is an ongoing component to the cycle of learning to improvise.

## 3. Synergy

Teamwork is yet another way to become better at improvisation. I encourage improvisers to become musicians who make everyone else look and sound better. Generosity is a critical skill one needs in order to be at the height of this art form. It is a collaborative medium after all, and if improvisers are not able or willing to work with others, then the art form itself will not function well. Everyone who is performing must believe in the idea that there is a valuing of the collective product over individual achievement. As a result of playing for many years, I discovered that successful improvisation-based performance ensembles must agree to a synergistic view. This view is one in which different parts cooperate advantageously towards the final objective. This means that it is not enough to think the whole is greater than the sum of the individual parts, but that the team will produce an overall better result than if each person were working toward the same goal individually. A synergistic view helps the improviser understand that every ensemble member plays a pivotal role.

## 4. Micromanagement and Macromanagement

When I improvise, I make sure that I can manage my thoughts in two different ways. I become better at improv when I can switch my thought function between micro and macro points of view. I know where it is appropriate to think as a composer (macro level) and where it is reasonable to think as a performer (micro level). One way I successfully manage my thought process is by micromanaging my role. Instrumental improvisers must be able to see their role in the composition and how their instrument can add a voice to the musical conversation. They must think about what notes they are creating and how those notes convey the idea they want to project.

Additionally, improvisers must manage their mind at a macro level. I like to think about the ability to macromanage the piece as if I were a composer hearing the piece as a whole—how it begins, develops, and ends. Consequently, it is important to take the notes created while in performer mode and ponder how those notes will help propel the overall purpose of the composition. The improviser's mind consistently switches back and forth between the micro and macro levels of artistic management.

## 5. Realization

I become better at improvisation when I realize that the same things that make good note readers make better, more competent, and confident real-time composers. Excellent note readers strive to have an artistic objective, reacting honestly to their surroundings.

An artistic objective is a critical part of the creative process, both when musicians practice by themselves and when they perform with others. I was a part of a team that created a completely improvised musical for children. When I needed to add music during the show, I would make sure I knew the objective. Then as I improvised the song, I made sure that everything I played centered around that objective. Goals in a composition are helpful for all involved and provide specificity in what can be a very broad, confusing environment. It can also serve as a way for individual musicians to evaluate where they are in the process of achieving the objective and how much further they need to go.

Improvisers who react honestly to their surroundings will create a space where music could spontaneously occur, pushing out the boundaries that hold them back from true freedom of expression. Artistic boundaries are good to have when first starting to improvise; however, I strive to find the truth in what I am performing and to break down the limitations in the process. I find that truth by listening intently to my surroundings and reacting in an honest, vulnerable way. I try to understand the historical significance of the piece and express a personal connection throughout a performance.

If there is nothing worth saying, then I will not enter the fray; however, if something needs to be said, I will respond truthfully with confidence and integrity. Good improvisers realize that they need to demonstrate through their instrument rather than verbalize a plan. Talking about an idea ahead of time or in the moment breaks the kind of communication that needs to happen within the mind for peak improvisational performance. I realize that I need to ignite the part of my intellect that communicates nonverbal communication.

## 6. Stepping into the Deep

It is easy to fall into tried and true patterns of improvisation, just as in life, where people choose to remain in environments that have been tested and proven to be comfortable. However, I endeavor to force myself into situations where I take on a role never played before to improve. For example, years ago, I performed in an improvising classical, contemporary chamber ensemble. One day in rehearsal, I recommended that the players who create the main thematic material experiment by performing more countermelodies, rhythmic driving patterns, or harmonic support.

Conversely, I suggested that those players who typically do not play the melody create the piece's main theme. Another example was when I was in a jazz combo rehearsal. I recommended that the drummer play the melody and all other group members figure out a way to support the drummer's melody. When improvisers go outside of their comfort zones, they discover so much more about themselves than if they had stayed in the same old musical roles and patterns.

## 7. Confidence

My experience has taught me that the best improvisers all have high levels of internalized confidence. This confidence is not arrogance—it is a self-assurance that creates behavior resulting in an environment where risk still happens but is limited to where both the performer and the audience are secure in knowing the end goal. Note that a healthy amount of nervous energy will not negatively impact performance. Improvisers can still have nervous energy before a performance. Still, they need to be at a place where the audience is not sharing in their nervousness. Both as a performer and as a music director, I have seen that confident improvisers listen more than they speak. They also, at times, evade the focus to let others excel. They are not afraid to be wrong or to look foolish. As a matter of fact, confident improvisers look at mistakes as an opportunity to grow and become better performers. A confident improviser recognizes when to lead and when to follow other players.

## 8. Genuine Study of the Craft

Great improvisers take the craft seriously. Improvisation is an art that demands respect. It requires taking the time to figure out how to improve when things do not go well. Genuine study of the craft also involves discovering how something works well when performed successfully, practicing concepts taught from classes, watching good improv, and doing improv with more experienced people. I have found in my own practice that it is critical to take the time to dive deeply into the mechanics of improvisation and take it seriously enough to critique and receive criticism, asking questions that will lead to more sophisticated levels of performance. As with any other art form, improvement takes time and dedication.

## 9. Practice

How does one get better at improvising if improvisation exists in an unknown state? Just like anything else in life, improvisation can improve the more times one experiences it. While it is true that improvisation exists, to a certain extent, in an unknown state during a performance, it is not true that a performing improviser doesn't prepare. An improviser will practice exercises, learn genre-specific stylistic approaches, rehearse with others, etc. The state of not knowing what the result will be or how one will get to the outcome may never change. Still, improvisers are ready for anything that may happen in the moment when it comes to performance because of their preparation.

They must also practice professionalism, for example, showing up on time, treating others with professional courtesy, coming to the rehearsal room ready, and being present in the moment. In order to be comfortable with real-time composition, the improviser must understand and practice improvising. Improvisation is more than just magically coming up with something on the spot. I learned early on that I had to practice the art of "being and doing in the moment" if I ever wanted to be competent in this field. Outside of practicing improvisation as a skill set, I also made sure that I improved fluency on my instrument. It is critical to have a moderate level of technical ability on your instrument before diving deep into compelling creative improvisational performance.

## 10. Imagination

Improvising does not necessarily always mean creating notes; rather, it is the act of creating something through imagination while executing it in real time. So, where does imagination come from? In his book *Effortless Mastery*, Kenny Werner says,

> The taming of the mind, the dissolution of the ego and the letting go of all fears can only evolve through patient practice. There is nothing worth attaining on this or any other planet that doesn't take practice. As you do this, you become aware of another space.

He goes on to say that "the inner space is the place where joy, pleasure, and fulfillment—worldly and otherwise—are available in unlimited supply." There is an unlimited supply of musical ideas that live inside the improviser's creative, imaginative mind. Even though there is an endless supply, improvisers must practice accessing this part of the mind—where intention breeds. Begin by understanding the importance of calming the conscious mind (intellect) in order to access the creative, imaginative mind. I have discovered the key to the door that grants access to the creative, imaginative mind is to, as Werner says, practice letting go of all fears and dissolve the ego.

Additionally, when improvisers use their imagination, it is crucial not to label ideas as either good or bad; instead, just let them flow through without judgment. In every instance of improvisation, I seek to bring my imagination to the fore. If imagination was a crossroad, it would intersect with technique. The intersection of imagination and technique is an excellent laboratory for musical creation.

### *The Bottom Line*

> You must experience rain in order to experience the rainbow. Understand that with patience and practice, the "rainbow" will appear at the right time. The rain, in this case, is the process of taking classes, trying new ideas, working out dysfunctions, practicing, listening, analyzing past performances, etc. This work ethic grants access to a place where you can consciously push aside all of that previous labor and be in the moment of real-time composition (rainbow). The rainbow is the moment when the elements *trust*, *ability to listen*, *synergy*, *micro/macromanagement*, *realization*, *stepping into the deep*, *confidence*, *studying your craft*, *practice*, and *imagination* coalesce to the point of spontaneity. Once the rainbow appears, you can choose which color (genre) you like best and focus more intently on it.

### *Why Improvise?*

No matter how much you plan, occasionally, things do not turn out the way you wanted them to turn out. What do you do in this situation? Can you make adjustments in the moment or give into fear and disappointment? Studying improvisation can help. If you have avoided music

6   *The Essential Elements*

improvisation because of the fear of the unknown, you're not alone. Many have evaded the study of improvisation due to any number of reasons, including the lack of exposure or fear of making a mistake. This is understandable; however studying improvisation will teach you how to make adjustments in moments of perceived chaos. It can also help you make interpretive choices with repertoire. This is because improvisation requires you to pick apart the elements of a composition and apprehend the ability to construct a piece of music. The study of improv has also helped me reinforce focus in the practice room and develop my musical ear.

As I reflect on how the study of improvisation has impacted my life, I realized that the effects of improv had both a musical impact and one that transcended musicianship skills. I recognized myself as being affected in ten ways: 1) obtained a better global perspective, 2) amplified the creative thought process, 3) boosted listening skills, 4) increased sight-reading abilities, 5) improved "outside the box" thinking, 6) developed better change management engagement, 7) facilitated more efficient collaboration, 8) strengthened the willingness to change my mind, 9) enhanced resilience, and 10) heightened state of awareness.

---

**Ten Effects of Improvisation**

1. Global View
2. Creative Inspiration
3. Listening Intensifies
4. Enhanced Note Reading
5. The Possible Impossible Idea
6. Change Management
7. Collaboration
8. Sunk Cost Fallacy
9. Failure
10. Shifting Mindsets

---

### Effect 1: Global View

Improvisation pushed me to develop open-mindedness and think in a broader, more global mindset. As a result of improvisation study, I consider issues from a global perspective. Why? The improviser's job is to create something that no one has heard before while performing it for and with others. With a more open mind, I learned to see a piece or situation as a whole, not just from my own perspective. Thus, I became a better more active team member in the creative process.

### Effect 2: Creative Inspiration

Daily practice of musical improvisation inspires creativity. The innovative nature of improvisation will affect the desire to experiment. As I practiced creating new ideas daily, I noticed a fearlessness within myself that sought new ways to advance my musical ideas. Coupled with an open mind, I dove into not just considering new ideas but trying them out. These ideas may not always be the best, but creative people are willing to investigate and put them to the test.

### Effect 3: Listening Intensifies

I discovered that daily practice of musical improvisation intensified my capacity to listen with intention. Since listening is a crucial factor in learning to improvise, it makes sense that one's listening abilities would improve. What I also noticed is that I listened to pre-composed music differently. I listen more intently to both the broad scheme of the musical composition, such as quality of sound, harmonic progressions, form, as well as the minutia of musical elements such as articulation, phrasing, dynamics, etc. Listening at this level has also helped develop pitch matching and memorization skills. While the primary effect is how one listens to music, I intensely listen outside of music. I also found myself better at listening to other people, empathizing with them, and engaging in deep, meaningful conversations to know them better.

### Effect 4: Enhanced Note Reading

I became a better note reader. Enhanced note reading was a result of constant micro- and macromanaging an improvised piece. When I improvise, I think of all the same aspects of music a composer would ponder—such as dynamics, articulation, form, harmonic progression, melodic contour, rhythmic patterns, style, etc. As I developed this ability, I was better able to 1) anticipate where a piece was going as I sight-read and 2) understand what a composer was trying to convey in a rehearsed piece.

### Effect 5: The Possible Impossible Idea

I have become very comfortable knowing that my ideas are not precious. As a result, I recognized that I have an infinite capability to create new ideas. I accepted the notion of the possible impossible idea. The possible impossible idea stems from an "outside the box" thought process while improvising music. Some musicians may dismiss outright an idea as impossible before considering it fully. Still, an improvising musician will say, "Yes and . . ." There is something priceless about "yes and-ing" a seemingly impossible or impractical idea. By saying yes to an idea and then chasing it down a path for a while, I forced myself to ask questions about what I am doing and where I am going musically. As a result, my improvisations improved. I realized that saying "yes and . . ." could lead somewhere genuinely interesting that I may not have considered initially.

### Effect 6: Change Management

Change management is navigating dynamic and chaotic environments. For example, non-musically, suppose a person is in a time of transition. In that case, improv can teach how to allow the mind to be agile enough to shift paradigms. As a result, I understood that whatever plan I had is now obsolete because the environment changed. Musically, I became better at assessing what is happening with the form rhythmically, melodically, harmonically, etc. in the moment, so, should a problem arise, I can move in a different direction rather than stick to a failing plan. For example, if I got lost in the changes, I became more comfortable with embracing what is needed to transform along with my surroundings.

*8  The Essential Elements*

### *Effect 7: Collaboration*

Collaboration is enabling another person to operate jointly to accomplish a collective artistic purpose. Improvisation forced me to trust more in the collective creative process. It pushed me to depend on others in whom I might not feel a lot of inherent trust, but I do it for the sake of the music. I discovered my listening skills deepened as I constantly focused on what others around me were playing. I became comfortable with not always trying to fill the space with my sound, trusting others in the group will contribute to the musical conversation.

### *Effect 8: Sunk Cost Fallacy*

The sunk cost fallacy is a previous expenditure that has already been paid and cannot be recouped in business. It requires a person to complete the project even though there is no return on the investment. Think of it as a situation where someone finishes the ill-fated project solely because he invested so many resources into doing it. Improvisation helps avoid this problem. In improv, there are no sunken costs. Why is this true? Jon Faddis told me in a masterclass, "There is no time in the moment of an improvised performance for a person to hold onto an idea until it works." I learned in that masterclass that I must make adjustments and divest myself of any investment in an idea, especially if it doesn't work. I also learned that it is ok to stop a solo if I don't have anything else to say musically.

### *Effect 9: Failure*

Within the walls of many different academic, athletic, and artistic fields, some live by the motto "Failure is not an option." Through improvisation, I learned to understand and embrace that failure is an option. Improv taught me the idea that failure is not what is important. It is how I recover from the failure that matters. Through a prolonged study of improvisation, I learned that mistakes should never define a person; instead, they should let mistakes refine who they are. There were many times throughout my course of study where I failed. Not only did I fail, but in the beginning stages, I failed more times than I succeeded. I credit the years of practicing improvisation with helping me to embrace the idea that the more mistakes I make, the better the player I become.

### *Effect 10: Shifting Mindsets*

I like to think that I have two types of mindsets when I engage in improvisation. The first is a mindset that allows for studying technique, analyzing mistakes and successes, practicing exercises, learning theory, reading sheet music, etc. The other is a mindset that forgets all of the technique and engages in a heightened performance flow.

In trying to unstitch the thread of intentional creativity, Dr. Charles Limb, an otolaryngologist who studies how musical creativity works in the brain, said in a 2008 *Hopkins Medicine Magazine* article, "During improv, the brain deactivates the area involved in self-censoring, while cranking up the region linked with self-expression. Essentially, a musician shuts down his inhibitions and lets his inner voice shine through." This statement makes sense to me. Improvisers who create something new while performing it may have nervous energy before a show. However, they do not let fear inhibit the ability to create during the performance, instead turn the inhibitions into freedom where ideas can freely flow.

In his 2010 TED Talk, Dr. Limb said,

> We think that at least a reasonable hypothesis is that, to be creative, you should have this weird dissociation in your frontal lobe. One area turns on, and a big area shuts off, so that you're not inhibited, you're willing to make mistakes, so that you're not constantly shutting down all of these new generative impulses.

Dr. Limb also suggests that during the act of improvisation, the area of the brain involving senses ignited, indicating a heightened state of awareness.

So, with all of benefits attributed to improvisation, coupled with basic elements needed to create musical spontaneity, how can musicians reap the reward improvisation has to offer? How can musicians develop the improviser mindset? How can a musician unlock the secret of knowing how to improvise and what to improvise? The answer is understanding the connection between intention and invention. What follows is a sequential approach to teaching and learning the skills needed to engage in improvisation.

# 2 Hear What to Play

## An Introduction to Intention

Having stated in the previous chapter the benefits of and essential skills for improvisation, it is crucial to shed light on action steps in how to gain insight into the art form. This insight centers on the connection between intention *(how* to improvise) and invention *(what* to improvise). The following few chapters will examine a pedagogical approach to bring out a musician's improvisatorial nature, or the *how* to improvise, regardless of style.

In this section:

1. Most novice improvisers may not understand how to access the mind's ear. Begin by introducing and understanding the concept of *intention*.
2. Work through simple exercises that will help bring out the power of intention and develop the mind's ear.
3. The next step is about taking the ability to conceive a thought and narrow the focus to musical thoughts.
4. Work through simple exercises that will help bring out the mind's musical ear, or *music intention*.
5. Continue to narrow the focus more by combining musical elements and igniting the improviser's imagination.
6. Work through fun exercises to develop soloistic imagination and group mind collaboration applications of intention.

This is a section that helps gain skill to learn how to conceive ideas, develop ideas into musical ideas, and then exploring how to use the mind's ear in a nonthreatening beginning improv ensemble. The goal for this section is to prepare musicians' intention skills so they can be better prepared for playing (communicating) as a soloist and with other musicians. In latter chapters of the book, we will take the skills learned in this section and center our attention to conceiving more focused musical ideas, and learning what to play (invention) to create a coherent solo.

Improvisation for many artists is unknown territory. Musicians may encounter improvisation through performing several different musical genres, such as baroque music, contemporary classical music, musical theater, liturgical services, orchestral pops concerts, jazz, rock, improv comedy, country, etc.; however, they may not understand how to improvise. Regardless of one's view on how improvisation should be used in art, experiencing improvisation may put the performer in a state of not knowing, which can be overwhelming. Experience teaching has shown me that when students tackle improvising in any style, they struggle with two main problems—knowing what to play and the act of improvisation itself, regardless of style.

DOI:10.4324/9781003341857-2

My pedagogical philosophy comes from a desire to develop a mechanism that can help any musician learn to improvise. My approach is to combat the absurd yet commonly held notion that improvisation can only be understood and enacted by a small subset of people with exceptional musical abilities. My philosophy is rooted in first focusing on how to translate an idea into a reality versus first focusing on knowing what to play within the context of the musical genre. My model is a unique, valuable approach because understanding how to translate an idea into a reality is the core concept that makes a great improviser. This concept transcends any one particular genre. Musicians could become overwhelmed with creating something out of nothing. If this is you, take a step back and think about improvisation as a process to create and not solely about understanding the music theory behind it.

So, what is improvisation? It is the instant simultaneous creation and implementation of music. More importantly, how does one engage in the act of improvisation regardless of a specified style? I always encourage my students to begin studying improvisation by acknowledging that they have a unique ability to place value on a sound they hear, perceive that sound as music, and express that music to others. They have also developed a sense of aural perception that allows for the ability to generate an original musical idea instantly. But how is this achieved successfully?

During my first year of teaching, my method was to begin with a genre focus and explain *what* to improvise—for example, telling students what notes to play over what chord. Over many years of teaching, I discovered that this common approach does a disservice, at first, to developing improvisers because it does not give them the skill set needed to create out of nothing, the very foundation of improvisation. It *only* gives them notes to play, rather than that essential process to create notes.

When I teach now, I begin by first focusing on *how* to improvise by setting an improvisatorial foundation. Learners must develop the ability to hear what they want to play, identify what was conceived mentally (the intervals, articulation, etc.), and then translate this through their instrument. The idea for the chapters in this section is to focus the musician's attention on developing the ability to create an idea. In later chapters, the musician will work toward transcribing that idea into a coherent solo. Subsequently, as musicians build a stronger improvisatorial foundation through a series of layered exercises, they can begin to construct a more coherent, compelling solo that will eventually become more genre-specific. The first step in my pedagogical approach to improvisation is to start by examining and developing a process I characterize as the *intention*.

## Mentally Conceive an Idea—the Intention

As I said earlier, improvisation is the instant simultaneous creation and implementation of music. Novice improvisers need to develop their capacity to create new ideas. So, step one of my three-pronged approach is what I have labeled the *intention* or mentally conceiving a musical idea. How, then, does one mentally conceive an idea? The answer is by tapping into a heightened level of awareness.

Barry J Kenny and Martin Gellrich, in the Science and Psychology of Music Performance, discuss the idea of two pedagogical approaches to teaching improvisation—deliberate practice and transcendence. According to them,

transcendence can be understood as a heightened state of consciousness that moves beyond the confines of the accumulated knowledge base itself. It is a state of consciousness that, like

12  *Hear What to Play*

deliberate practice, can be encouraged and cultivated at the outset of an improviser's development; it need not be delayed until the final stages of an artist's development.

So, how does one tap into a heightened state of awareness? I have used the following exercises as a first step to help heighten awareness.

*Awareness Exercises*

### Exercise 1: *Countdown breaths*

- *Find a quiet place.*
- *Sit down.*
- *Close your eyes.*
- *Take in a large breath through your nose.*
- *Slowly exhale as you count down from ten.*
- *Try it again and notice how your heart rate slows to the tempo of your countdown.*

### Exercise 2: *Asking questions*

- *Find a quiet place.*
- *Close your eyes.*
- *Do one countdown breath.*
- *Then mentally ask yourself one question.*
- *Repeat this cycle a few times or as needed.*

When you are asking questions, do not try to seek the answer. This exercise is not about finding solutions; it is about developing a higher level of awareness. Each question should lead to either a broader question or a more detailed question.

For example:

1. Broad direction: Who composed that baroque piece I heard recently?—followed by Was it baroque music?—followed by What is music?
2. Detailed direction: What are bugs? What bugs did I see today? How many legs did they have? What color were their legs?

Remember that after each question, instead of trying to find an answer, take a big breath through your nose and slowly exhale, counting down from ten. Then after a few rounds of asking questions followed by countdown breaths, open your eyes, stand up, and take thirty seconds to walk around the room, stretch, or get a drink of water. Then come back to the same spot and move on to Exercise 3.

### Exercise 3: *In one ear and out the other*

- *Find a quiet place.*
- *Sit down.*
- *Close your eyes.*
- *Do one countdown breath.*
- *Then allow thoughts to enter your mind, but do not focus on them.*

Allow thoughts to exit as easily as they entered. Do not try to control or achieve anything. These can be any thoughts—no need to connect them or go in any particular direction. Just accept them and then let them go. If you find your mind moving through a thought loop where you cannot let something go, go back to Exercise 1 and do a couple of countdown breaths.

The more time I spent on these exercises, the more I could center my mind toward the process of creation—not necessarily creating a new idea at first but rather constructing a state of mind that allows for peak creativity. I would recommend only doing these exercises for a few minutes each day at first and then adding more time as needed.

### *What Is Music?*

My experience with these exercises led me to ask questions such as "If the goal is to improvise music, then what is the definition of music?" "What is it that I am actually creating?" Since the perception of music can shift, defining music becomes a difficult task. The definition of music is limited because it states something that consistently redefines itself and has limitless form. Therefore, it is safe to say that music is easier to *describe* than *define*. Once individuals within a time period define music, a future generation will inevitably revolutionize that definition. As Irving Godt notes in his article *Music: a practical definition*, "Definitions, like fashions, change with time."

With the perception of music consistently changing and therefore altering its definition, how can I *describe* music so it can transcend time, culture, level of intelligence, and artistic taste? Answer: Music is when a listener places value on an experience created by a composer. I believe music carves itself in two parts: the "making of" music and the "listening to" music. When I improvise music, the experience created typically involves an idea I first mentally heard or conceived. I then begin the process of translating that idea into something that physically manifests the concept into music. During that performance, a listener places a value on the experience created by the improviser.

This value can take shape and be measured by any number of experiences as created by the listener's imagination or perception—where the listener is either the performer listening back to herself, another improvising musician, or the audience receiving the musical thought. The individual experiences affecting the value listeners place on the music include but are not limited to

1) the conceived intent of the performer listening back to herself
2) a nonverbal dialogue between performing musicians
3) a felt emotional response of a nonperforming listener
4) an experience of art for art's sake

The improviser who develops a deeper understanding of music recognizes that, at its core, the creation of music involves both the "making of" and the "listening to." Therefore, when improvisers create music, they are doing so to communicate an idea to a listener. Mentally conceiving an idea is as straightforward as thinking about what needs to be said to another person. But how can we achieve this musically?

### *Music Intention*

How can soloists utilize seemingly non-music-related exercises to develop a capacity to create new ideas in a musical realm? If mentally conceiving an idea is as straightforward as

14 *Hear What to Play*

thinking about what needs to be said to another person, then how can an improviser mentally conceive a musical idea? Does it work the same way? To help find the answer to this question, I recommend going deeper and answering the question: *What makes an excellent musical idea?*

It is safe to say that taste in music is subjective; however, improvisers must be careful in labeling some music as good and some as bad. In Jan LaRue's *Guidelines for Style Analysis*, he says that *subjective evaluation should never stop with such primitive determinations as "good/bad," or "best/worst," or "I like/dislike." For one thing, there are many kinds and periods of music, all of which include good things: we do not need to pursue a restrictive "best of all," ignoring the rest of music.* This is an important point because an improviser can learn a great deal from being exposed to all types of music. As a beginning improviser, be open to a wide variety of musical genres and ideas. What components are needed for a musical idea? I assert that a musical idea is a combination of subjective and objective components. As LaRue states, *[Composers] prepare for self-expression (subjective achievement) by intensive study of objective "rules" and practices originally derived from earlier composers.*

### What Elements Are Used to Create a Piece of Music?

The key to developing an increased capacity to improvise at this stage is to isolate and exercise fundamental elements of music. The most common objective ingredients to musical ideas are harmony, melody, and rhythm. Most of the time, elements of harmony, melody, and rhythm interact and generate memorable musical content. Improvisers use these elements to help determine the character of the music, the period, and the style.

---

**Fundamental Elements to Use When Developing a Capacity to Create Musical Ideas**

| Melody | Harmony | Dynamics |
|--------|---------|----------|
| Rhythm | Articulation | Form |

---

Through developing a heightened sense of awareness, I have found success in mentally conceiving music. This sense can be exercised and improved upon. I've always felt that the music I improvise is more spontaneous and organic if it originates from the mind's ear rather than a construct derived from written theory. Springboarding off the exercises discussed earlier, I suggest using the following activities that develop a heightened level of awareness. These Music Intention Exercises will help develop a capacity to create musical ideas.

### Countdown Breaths

Altering the countdown breath exercises, breathe in and out deeply over four steady beats (beats per measure should hover around 60). Think of a simple melody such as "Twinkle Twinkle Little Star" (or any simple tune), mentally sing that tune while exhaling, and notice one musical element of the tune, for example, the melodic contour. Then do it again and focus on a different musical aspect of the tune, such as the rhythm. Only pay attention to one musical component at a time. Then as you circle through isolating elements such as melody, rhythm, harmony, articulation, dynamics, and form mentally, take a short break. After the break, play "Twinkle Twinkle Little Star" (or any simple tune) on your instrument exactly how you heard it in your head. No written music is allowed.

**Asking Questions**

Breathe in for four counts and then out for four counts, then ask yourself one question. Allow that one question to lead you to a more profound question. Let each cycle of inquiry lead to another question that leads to a more in-depth question. When you are asking questions, do not try to seek the answer. This exercise is not about finding solutions; it is about developing a higher level of awareness. Each question should lead to either a broader question or a more detailed question.

**Melodic**

Musically: instead of questions, replace a question with one note.

1) Focus your mind on hearing an original melody. The melody can be as long or as short as you would like. I would recommend very short melodies.
2) Hear the first note of the melody in your head. Listen for the length of the note, the pitch of the note, the dynamic of the note, etc.
3) Before moving on to another note in the melody, make sure that you can hear the exact note you want to play next. This is done by mentally singing the next note.
4) Mentally sing the whole melody.
5) Verbally sing the whole melody.
6) Play the melody on your instrument.

In this example, I hear a three-note melody. I focus on listening to the pitch of the first note in my head and identifying it as a G. I hear the G as a mezzo forte two beats long. I mentally sing the remaining notes in my melody, here again focusing on the details of how I want the note to sound.

Note that while rhythm and time and other musical elements are essential to the creation of a melody, as a beginner, it is important to eliminate as many factors as possible to help better focus the mind and develop a connection to the instrument. As you progress, you can always add more advanced musical components.

Once you have mentally conceived the note(s) you want to play, play that note(s) on your instrument. If what comes out of your instrument does not match what you heard in your head, go back and simplify your musical thoughts. Perhaps your melody is only two notes. At this point, that is ok! You are developing melodic intention—the ability to hear a note(s) you want to play before you play it on your instrument.

**Rhythmic**

Musically: instead of questions, replace a question with one rhythm. This is a rhythmic intention exercise, so your focus should only be on rhythm.

1) Focus your mind on listening for an original rhythm. The rhythm can be as long or as short as you would like. I would recommend very short rhythmic fragments.
2) Listen for the length of each rhythm, the tempo, the dynamics, etc.
3) Mentally sing the whole rhythm.
4) Verbally sing the whole rhythm.
5) Play the rhythm on your instrument.

In this example, I hear a small rhythmic fragment, in this case four eight notes and two quarter notes. I focus on the tempo, the length of each note, and visualize the exact rhythm. I mentally sing the rhythmic fragment, here again focusing on the details of how I want the rhythm to sound. I strive to make sure I play exactly what I hear in my head.

Once you have mentally conceived the rhythm you want to play, play that rhythm on your instrument. If what comes out of your instrument does not match what you heard in your head, go back and simplify your musical thoughts. Perhaps your rhythm is four quarter notes. At this point, that is ok! You are developing rhythmic intention—the ability to hear a rhythm you want to play before you play it on your instrument.

**Harmonic**

Musically: instead of questions, replace a question with one harmony. This is a harmonic intention exercise, so your focus should only be on harmony.

1) Focus your mind on listening for a harmony. If this is too much of a challenge, play a simple triad on the piano to give yourself some context.
2) Mentally sing the outline of the triad.
3) Verbally sing the outline of the triad.
4) Play the outline of the triad on your instrument.

In this example, I hear a C major triad. I mentally sing each note of the chord followed by singing it out loud. Finally, I play the outlined chord.

As you progress, challenge yourself by not using a piano as an aid. Also, increase the number of chords. For example: go through the same steps as before for additional chords in the exercise.

Once you have mentally conceived the harmony you want to play, play that harmony on your instrument. If what comes out of your instrument does not match what you heard in your head, go back and simplify your musical thoughts. Perhaps the harmony is only two notes (root and third). At this point, that is ok! You are developing harmonic intention—the ability to hear a harmony you want to play before you play it on your instrument.

**Articulation**

Musically: instead of questions, replace a question with one articulation. This is an articulation intention exercise, so your focus should only be on articulation.

1) Focus your mind on listening for a very specific articulation. Staccato, legato, marcato, accent, accent with a legato marking, etc.
2) Mentally sing the articulation.
3) Verbally sing the articulation.
4) Play the articulation on your instrument.

In this example, I hear one note (G) with an accent. I mentally sing the accented note followed by singing it out loud. Finally, I play the note.

As you progress, make sure to practice the various types of articulation. Then I would encourage you to mix and match a variety of different articulations. Remember to listen with purpose, then sing and then play.

Once you have mentally conceived the articulation you want to play, play that articulation on your instrument. If what comes out of your instrument does not match what you heard in your head, go back and simplify your musical thoughts. You are developing articulation intention—the ability to hear an articulation you want to play before you play it on your instrument.

**Dynamics**

Musically: instead of questions, replace a question with one dynamic. This is a dynamic intention exercise, so your focus should only be on dynamics.

1) Focus your mind on listening for a very specific dynamic. Forte, piano, mezzo forte, etc.
2) Mentally sing the dynamic.

3) Verbally sing the dynamic.
4) Play the dynamic on your instrument.

In this example, I hear one note (G) that is forte. I mentally sing the forte note followed by singing it out loud. Finally, I play the note exactly as I hear it.

As you progress, make sure to practice the various types of dynamics. Then I would encourage you to mix and match a variety of different dynamics. Remember to listen, then sing and then play.

Once you have mentally conceived the dynamic you want to play, play that dynamic on your instrument. If what comes out of your instrument does not match what you heard in your head, go back and simplify your musical thoughts. You are developing dynamic intention—the ability to hear a dynamic you want to play before you play it on your instrument.

**Form**

This exercise isn't so much about form as it is about training your mind to mix and match different elements in a particular order.

1) Pick and choose from the previous elements of music: melody, rhythm, harmony, articulation, dynamics.
2) Mentally conceive a form using your selected components. For example: rhythm, dynamics, melody, rhythm.
3) In the first section, mentally conceive a rhythm and play that rhythm. For example:

4) Then move on to playing that rhythm in a particular dynamic or series of dynamics.

5) The third section follows by adding new melodic notes to the rhythm.

6) The final section goes back to the original note and the original rhythm.

7) Remember to always hear it, sing it, and then play it.

## *In One Ear and Out the Other*

I have often found that students (a) have cluttered ideas in their head, (b) have difficulty transcribing what they hear, and (c) have a hard time focusing. Then when they try to play something on their instrument, the notes are jumbled, and it does not adequately represent what they want. Try not to get discouraged; this is a natural part of the learning process. Students need to develop their capacity to create new ideas by developing the mind-instrument connection. The "In One Ear and Out the Other" exercise can help with this.

1. Hear a simple melody—the exact pitches of that melody, and the precise rhythm of that melody, etc.
2. If more than one melody enters your brain or it continues for a long period of time or it becomes a little too complicated, let it go. Eliminate the mental clutter. Start over and simplify.
3. Focus your mind on going deeper into the details of one simple short melodic idea, and work toward verbally transcribing this simple melody precisely as you hear it. To start, no more than two bars in length.
4. Once you are able to sing the melody in your head, then sing it out loud.
5. When you are able to sing the melody out loud exactly how you hear it, then play it on your instrument.

It would be best if you did not write anything down—only play it on your instrument by ear!

The focus of this exercise should be to develop a capacity to create and transcribe your musical thoughts without the aid of sheet music. During the early stage of development, consider any note that comes out of the instrument successful if it matches what you first hear in your mind.

> Know that your mentally conceived melodies can take any shape or form—at least at this point. The melodies do not have to be award-winning masterpieces. They can be two notes, or perhaps one note repeated with various articulations. Think of it as being taught how to develop a recipe for food consumption. At this point, you are using basic ingredients (melody, dynamics, articulation) as a tool to help develop skills in mixing and baking. In future chapters, we will examine in more detail how to incorporate the right ingredients, that is, to create coherent solos and make better musical choices.

Most non-improvising musicians typically follow a pre-composed piece of music practiced individually and then well-rehearsed before a formal concert. A conductor who determines the piece's artistic dimensions dictates the concert and its preceding rehearsals. However, what if

20    *Hear What to Play*

the traditional idea of how these musicians experience music just scratches the surface? What if, whether in a non-conducted chamber ensemble or conducted symphonic setting, classical musicians, and for that matter any musician, understand that they are constantly improvising? And if so, what sort of exercises are available to help bring out an improvisatorial nature in a performing musician, both as a soloist and a member of an ensemble?

### *Essential Elements for Intention*

### 1. Trust

Trust in the process not in the product—at least at this point. Right now, you want to establish an open mind to better receive and create ideas. Trust that the exercises will help you gain a heightened sense of awareness. Trust in the idea that the beginning stages are about the development of a musician's capacity to create new ideas, and transcribe those ideas through the instrument—not necessarily the ability to implement complicated bebop lines over rhythm changes or to transcribe the masters—at least not yet!

### 2. Listen

Listen to your inner voice. Ignore your inner critic. Since this stage in the learning process is more about the process to create an open mind, there is no need for a critic, since there is no tangible compelling solo one should focus on. Listen to your inner voice, the voice that is leading you toward higher consciousness. As a reminder: heightening your level of awareness may not directly help you understand, for example, how to improvise a solo over Giant Steps at first. However, it will help you become more in tune with your surroundings (harmony, rhythm, etc.) from the ensemble and your ability to hear all aspects of your mentally generated melody.

### 3. Synergy

Create synergy with your breaths. In the countdown breaths exercise, focus your mind on how you are taking in and releasing your breath. As you countdown, learn to synergize your countdown with your breath. Create synergy with yourself. Imagine that you are both listener and performer. Be very clear with your musical intent. Be an active listener to what is created mentally. Then as a performer, match the mental sound through your instrument in real time.

### 4. Micromanagement and macromanagement

The broad direction asking questions exercise can help you begin to develop a sense of macromanagement skills, and the detailed direction asking questions exercise can help begin to develop micromanagement skills. Remember that the more you practice these exercises, the more you will want to think on both the macro and the micro level. As you hear the sound you will eventually play on your instrument, make sure to listen intently to where you are in the moment as well as where you want to go in the future. Think of the notes you play in the present as always in motion—the notes you are playing just came from notes you just performed and will lead to new notes in the future.

### 5. Realization

Understand that it is ok if your mind starts to wander and you feel these exercises are not helping you. Realize that studying improvisation takes a long time to learn. Just stop and try again. Or perhaps it is time to take a break and come back to it later. Realize and understand that this chapter is about developing intention. The idea is to develop the ability to hear a musical element(s) mentally. These elements do not need to be fully formed melodies, complicated rhythms, or complex harmonies. The simpler the element, the better! At least for now.

## 6. Stepping into the deep

You might not be a person that has ever tried exercises like this . . . that's ok! You are probably also the type of person that either a) has no experience with improvisation or b) has little experience with improvisation. In all cases, understand that trying something new may lead you to learn new things. It is ok to fail! Remember that you are trying something new. Stepping into the deep of new things takes time to learn and absorb. Be patient. This new experience will eventually become second nature.

## 7. Confidence

Have the confidence to know that after doing these exercises you will not automatically be able to improvise a solo over rhythm changes. Rather, be confident in that fact that in order for you to get different results, sometimes you'll have to approach things in a different way. Draw on what you already know. You have already played enough pre-composed written music to inform your musical mind. Have the confidence to know that at this point you will have enough musical material to draw upon. Here again, at least at this point!

## 8. Genuine study of craft

I always encourage my students to center themselves before a practice session or a performance. Before a session, allow yourself a few moments to clear your mind, taking deep breaths, and focus on the goals for the day. I have found that the more I incorporate these types of exercises on a daily basis, before a performance or practice session, the more focused and calm I am, the more focused and calm I am, the more productive I become.

## 9. Practice

A daily commitment a few minutes a day will help instill a mindfulness that could open new pathways for creative thoughts to enter into your mind. If you find yourself becoming bored with some of the music intention exercises, I would encourage you to dive deeper into a particular music element or elements. Then mix and match more elements together. Remember: you can always hear/play something shorter, longer, faster, slower, higher, lower, softer, and louder.

## 10. Imagination

For the asking questions exercise, use your imagination and come up with a variety of different topics to ask yourself. Or perhaps, for the music intention exercises, imagine the sound of whatever musical element you are working on. Now imagine it exactly how you want it to go. The more detailed your imagination, the easier it will be to hear what you want to play in the moment. Know, don't guess! Don't be surprised by what comes out of your instrument; be intentional in portraying exactly what you hear in your head.

# 3 Establish an Improvisational Mindset

How does one begin the process to create something not written on the page? How can one convey an artistic idea through musical language but in real time? The following exercises are not meant to instill a rigid, deep-rooted learning pattern, basing one's improvisation on a design that always exists. It intends to establish an environment where musicians can expand the creation process in real time through improvisational exercises.

To be clear, these etudes and the following group exercises are part of the learning process that brings out an improvisatorial nature. Learn to develop an improvisational nature, and later mold that nature into a coherent solo. As a reminder, developing the *how* is a precursor to learning the *what*. So, before diving into constructing a solo, it is important to explore ways to bring out an improvisational disposition.

## Imagination Etudes

Over the course of teaching varying degrees of students, I discovered that imagination etudes are a helpful way to develop a unique sense of inspired artistry. Start small, and instead of focusing on what notes to play, utilize the imagination etude concept, which forces the creativity to dictate the melodic construction. I have narrowed down the imagination etudes I've created to three of the most effective. These three main etudes will help the musician bring out their innate ability to use their imagination. Each etude is more complex than the last.

### *Imagination Etude 1: What Is a Noun?*

*Part I: Describe*

A noun is a person, place, or thing. Begin this etude by picking a person, place, or thing. Describe, in words, this person, place, or thing in as much detail as possible, attempting not to leave out any detail.

For example:

> I imagine a man weighing 230 pounds with long, thick brown hair. He is 6 feet 5 inches tall with a large-built frame and a scar on his face from his days as a railroad worker.

DOI:10.4324/9781003341857-3

*Part II: Improvise a Soundtrack*

Once you describe a person, place, or thing, improvise a soundtrack on your instrument. Ask yourself what the soundtrack of this person, place, or thing is. This etude is short and should be no longer than a phrase or two. Imagine the soundtrack part to this etude being more like a leitmotif. For now, try not to over think the musical elements. Just imagine the picture you are creating in your head and try to represent that picture through sound.

For example:

> The improviser could play giant intervallic leaps to represent this man's large build and height. There could be heavy accents and loud dynamics to showcase the weight of the man. The improviser could perform longer valued notes to represent his long hair length. The improviser could end the etude with a quote from the American folk song "I've Been Working on the Railroad," representing this man as a railroad worker.

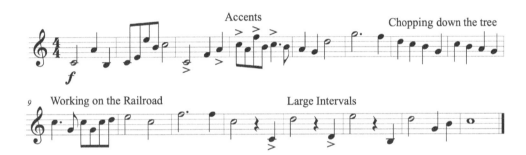

**Imagination Etude 2: Tell a Story**

*Part I: Describe*

Begin this etude by creating any type of short story. Be as detailed as possible when telling this story with words and write it so that nothing goes unnoticed.

For example:

> The story of two lovers, Sam and Della, from two quarreling houses, the Dusang house, and the Storpio house, is predestined to end in disaster. Sam and Della find ways to romance each other until the relationship is exposed. Upon discovering the relationship, tragic events occur between the two families, resulting in the ultimate death of the couple. In the end, the two families, stricken with grief, put their differences aside and work to begin a peaceful resolution.

*Part II: Improvise a Soundtrack*

Once there is a story created, you must now improvise a soundtrack on your instrument. Ask yourself, what is the soundtrack of this story? This etude is more enlarged, more involved, and

24   *Establish an Improvisational Mindset*

an extension of Imagination Etude No. 1. In addition to musically describing a person, place, or thing, this is where the improviser would musically describe the sound of each section of the story and how each section connects to the next. The improviser must also show how the music echoes the story's development and how the completion of the music echoes the ending of the story. Once again, try not to overthink the musical elements. Just imagine the story you are creating in your head, and try to represent that story through sound.

For example:

> In the story of Sam and Della, the improviser could begin by improvising a leitmotif for Della and then one for Sam. As the story transitions, that is, the romance is discovered, the music should represent that shift. If a person discovered something that she did not like, what would the sound be of that something? Perhaps it could be the use of chromatics. Then as the tragic events occur, the improvised music needs to be reflective of these tragic events—perhaps notes with a rhythmic percussive quality. This could be followed by a funeral music section and finally a transition to an ending as the two families reconcile. This reconciliation could be represented musically by shifting to a major tonality, slowing down the tempo, or lowering the dynamics.

*Imagination Etude 3: See the Color, Play the Color*

*Part I: Describe*

Begin this etude by picking a color. This color is not attached to a person, place, or thing. It is literally just an envisioned color. What sort of descriptive words would I use to describe this color? Think about the selected color and be able to answer the following questions.
For example:

| | |
|---|---|
| What is the color? | blue |
| If it's blue, what kind of blue? | dark blue |
| Does the color represent a feeling? | sadness |
| Does this color have a texture, and if so, what is the consistency? | thick like molasses |

*Part II: Improvise a Soundtrack*

Keep your mind focused on the selected color and improvise a soundtrack. Ask yourself what sounds would represent the color chosen. How will the answers to my questions be best conveyed through my instrument? Here again, try not to overthink the musical elements. Just imagine what your chosen color would sound like, and try to represent that color through your instrument.
For example:

I would begin in Bb and center my tonality around the Bb pentatonic scale. I would play very slowly with as dark of a sound I could create. I would add occasional chromatic passing tones to represent the darkness of the blue. And alter tonalities between major pentatonic and minor pentatonic to represent the multilayers of feeling sad.

**Additional thoughts:** For each of the previous imagination etudes, there is no right or wrong with your musical choices. The goal of these etudes is to develop a personal sense of creativity and nonverbal communication skills. It is about leading with your imagination skills and translating images through your instrument. Coherent compelling solo construction will be discussed in later chapters. For an added challenge, I would recommend the improviser perform these etudes in front of someone, asking them to answer the question: *What is the noun? What story am I trying to tell? What color am I playing?* And seeing how close their answer matches yours.

## Group Mind Exercises

I once was a part of a quartet of contemporary orchestral chamber musicians who regularly performed entirely improvised concerts. One event, in particular, stands out. We were performing in East Harlem. The opening piece began with the double bass player improvising a Latin style bass line. The trombone entered, playing an improvised main melody. I then joined on trumpet with a supportive countermelody. The piccolo player, Mary, waited for several iterations of the form to pass and then added high fast motifs, trills, and sweeping scale flourishes.

What if the goal was to have more than one musician improvise at the same time? How was this contemporary classical chamber ensemble able to improvise an entire concert? Why did Mary wait for such a long time before she entered? Why did she decide to play high fast motifs, trills, and sweeping scale flourishes? What talent did Mary and the rest of her fellow chamber musicians have that made it possible to create a piece of music without discussing it first? It was not talent; it was exercising improvisational techniques that help to develop a group mind thought process. The following exercises help to create an improvisational group mind.

Here again, developing the *how to improvise* is a precursor to learning *what to improvise*. So, before diving into *what to play*, it is important to explore ways to bring out an improvisational disposition.

### *Exercise I: Audience Input Exercise*

In this exercise, one person performs solo. The nonperformers provide the soloist with musical suggestions. For example, one nonperformer may suggest Eb, and another may recommend AABA form. Whatever the suggestion may be, the improvising soloist must create a work based on the suggestion. Ideally the suggestion should match the improviser's level of comfort and experience.

---

Examples of varying degrees of suggestions:

Level 1: play in Eb—player plays anything they are comfortable playing given their ability, as long as it is centered in the key of Eb

Level 2: play AABA form—player plays something: could be a melody, or a rhythmic pattern, or just a couple of notes without meter, or anything they are comfortable playing given their ability (A), then they play that something again (A)—make sure it is simple enough that whatever is played can be replicated. Then play something new and different (B). Then return to the original something played (A).

Level 3: Multiple suggestions at a time. Play in Eb, AABA, quarter notes only, etc.

---

*Other suggestions:* play quarter notes, play in ¾ time, play in the key of C#, only play arpeggios, play staccato, play only natural notes, play lyrically, only play on the offbeat.

*For a more challenging experience*: add additional members. So, instead of just a soloist, it is now a quartet, consisting of drums, piano, bass, and soloist, etc.

*Exercise II: One Note at a Time Exercise*

This exercise develops the ensemble's ability to share in the process of creating a musical line, but only one note at a time. The exercise begins with the improvisers in a circle; the first improviser plays one note, the next improviser plays the next note in the phrase, and the following improviser plays the third note in the phrase until the entire completed phrase comes to fruition. Once there is a completed phrase, a new phrase begins, here again, only one note at a time.

Please note:

> For beginners: Predetermine the meter, the tempo, and the length of the phrase. As the group of players advance, allow these parameters to be determined in the moment.

*Exercise III: Synergy Exercise*

This exercise aims for all players to develop a shared rhythmic and melodic synergism.

*Rhythmic Synergy*

Four or more improvisers are sitting with their backs toward each other. At the beginning of this exercise, the first improviser creates a rhythm.
For example:

The next improviser seated to the left of the first improviser plays the same rhythm but with different notes.
For example:

The third improviser plays the exact same rhythm as the second improviser but with different notes.

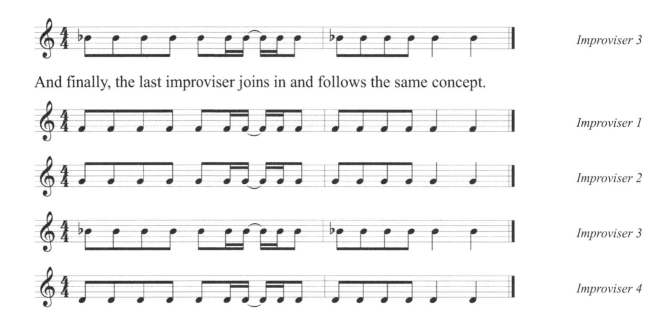

And finally, the last improviser joins in and follows the same concept.

## Melodic Synergy

Once all four improvisers play the same exact rhythm simultaneously, the first improviser plays a simple melodic motif that fits into the rhythmic ensemble groove.

The players all go around matching the same exact same melodic motif.

### Exercise IV: Sound Effects Exercise

There is no melody, rhythm, or harmony in this exercise, only sound effects. This exercise is about creating nonmusical sound effects to represent, in this example, a mechanical device.
  Example:

> A group of improvisers think of a mechanical device such as an airplane. Each member of the ensemble thinks of a way her instrument could sound like something associated with an airplane and then mimics that sound through her instrument.

Example of one musician (trombone) using slide to sound like a propellor:

At the end of this exercise, nonperforming ensemble musicians in the room should be able to guess the sound the performers were trying to portray.

30  *Establish an Improvisational Mindset*

### *Exercise V: Emotional Exercise*

Improvisers begin by pulling a piece of paper from a hat with an emotion written on it. The job of the improviser(s) is to play the emotion. The improvisation does not have to be within a certain meter or involve melody, rhythm, or harmony. It must, however, represent the chosen feeling. As the piece is improvised, have a nonperformer pull another piece of paper out of the hat. As the nonperformer shows the new feeling to the group (or individual), they must instantly switch and project the musical feeling selected. This exercise is a precursor to the more advanced call-and-react exercise. Think of this emotional exercise as being more about musically projecting a feeling and not about the technical elements of musicianship such as melody, harmony, or rhythm.

### *Exercise VI: Reflection Exercise*

The goal of this exercise is to develop a hive mind.

Level 1:

> Without any prior discussion, begin with two improvisers facing each other. They must attempt to play the same starting note without verbalizing which note. If they fail at the first attempt, continue until both improvisers can play the same note the first time simultaneously.

Level 2:

> Once the two improvisers are able to simultaneously play the same first note, they will attempt to play the same exact phrase. One improviser should be the leader and improvise a simple melodic motif and the other a follower. The goal is for the follower to anticipate the following note and rhythm of the leader. The leader must not try to mess up the followers. Instead, the leader should play something in a direction that the followers can anticipate. Eventually, the goal is to not be able to tell who is leading and who is following.

Level 3:

> Add more and more improvisers so that eventually, the whole ensemble can perform as one voice.

For more of a challenge, try these exercises:

### *Exercise I: Create a Phrase Exercise*

The key to this exercise is listening. It must involve two or more improvisers. The exercise begins with one person playing one measure of an improvised musical line. The second improviser continues that musical line, playing the second measure of the phrase. The third improviser plays the third measure. The fourth improviser follows by playing the fourth measure.

Notice how the last note of the first measure is a leading tone to the IV chord in measure two. Some of the best ways to connect one measure to the next in this exercise is to play either a half or whole step away from the previous note. For even more of a challenge, think about creating a simple chord progression like I V I or I IV V I, etc., and have each improviser for each measure play their fragment over a particular chord.

The goal of this exercise is for the ensemble to create a musical phrase that is seamless from one player to the next. Nonperforming musicians must listen and be ready to create their measure. Their measure must add to the phrase by coming out of the previous measure and leading to the next measure. Each improviser must develop the skill of listening and adding on items that help propel the music forward, rather than forcing their own agenda by performing whatever they want to play regardless of what occurs creatively in the moment.

*Exercise II: Lead Melody Support Melody Exercise*

Begin by having one improviser play a melody.

Then a second improviser improvises a different melody that supports the original line.

The first improviser stops playing and leaves. As the first improviser leaves, the new improviser enters. The new player plays a supporting melody to the second improviser.

32   *Establish an Improvisational Mindset*

As the second improviser leaves, a new improviser enters and plays a different melody in support of the third improviser, and so on and so forth.

Here are some tips to playing a supportive melody:

1. In general, if your main melody is held (half/whole notes), then your supportive melody should move (quarter/eighth notes)
2. Try fun ostinato patterns as seen in improviser three measure 5.
3. While the low G in the last two bars of improviser four's line may not seem like an ideal melody, it does put itself in a subordinate role of the main melody.
4. In terms of harmony, try to stick to either one chord throughout or a two-bar phrase consisting of the I chord and the V chord.
5. Be familiar with the chord tones of the key you choose.
6. Find the missing chord tone. Listen for any missing chord tones in the main melody. Then begin your supportive melody with that missing chord tone.
7. Find and fill any gaps. Listen to the main melody, and find pockets where the supportive melody can be heard on its own.
8. When the main melody ascends, the supportive line should descend and vice versa.

*Exercise III: Call and React Exercise*

The first part of this exercise focuses on elevating the musical environment, not necessarily on creating harmony, rhythm, or melody. Begin with two to four players from the ensemble.

Nonperforming ensemble members must call out commands. These commands can be items such as "forte," "mezzo piano," "staccato," "legato," "andante," "allegro," etc. In any case, when someone calls out a command, the performing players must focus their improvisation on the order.

For example, if the command is "staccato," everyone must play staccato with no legato notes. The goal is to train the group members to switch styles immediately and match each other's—in this case, staccato markings.

For more of a challenge, begin with two to four players from the ensemble—label one as the leader and the remaining improvisers as followers. The leader of the performing group begins by improvising a harmonic pattern (possible pianist or guitar player), the percussionist should create a rhythmic pattern, and the soloist improvises a melody. As this occurs, nonperforming members call out commands. For even more of a challenge, have other melodic players join in creating various supportive melodies.

With practice, the group as a whole should strive to decrease the time it takes to react to a called-out new idea.

*Exercise IV: Modulation Exercise*

In this exercise, the improvisers work on developing a group-mindedness toward changing harmony within a piece. The exercise begins with two or more musicians creating a piece with a predictable harmonic structure, for example, I-IV-V-I. Once the improvisation has been defined and the harmonic structure is secure, one of the improvisers (typically one who plays chords like a guitar or piano) should modulate to a new key. After the modulation, all other improvisers must transpose their lines to the new key. Modulation to new keys should happen several times in one piece. If chordal instruments are not available, the improviser providing the bass line or main melody should lead the modulation.

Level One: One musician improvises a rhythm with one chord, all others play around that chord. Chordal musician modulates chord, and others respond accordingly. Predetermine the meter, the tempo, and the length of the improvisation. Once the predetermined length of the improvisation has ended, the exercise begins again in a new key. As the group of players advance, allow these parameters to be determined in the moment.

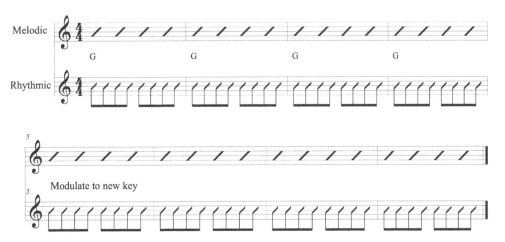

Level Two: One musician improvises a rhythm alternating between the tonic chord and the dominant chord—all others play around that chord. Chordal musician modulates chord, and others respond accordingly. Predetermine the meter, the tempo, and the length of the improvisation. Once the predetermined length of the improvisation has ended, the exercise begins again in a new key. As the group of players advance, allow these parameters to be determined in the moment.

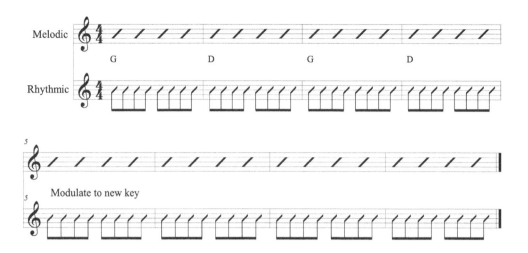

Level Three: Harmonic Structure: I IV V I. Increase the amount of chords that occur in the improv. Predetermine the meter, the tempo, and the length of the improvisation. Once the predetermined length of the improvisation has ended, the exercise begins again in a new key. As the group of players advance, allow these parameters to be determined in the moment.

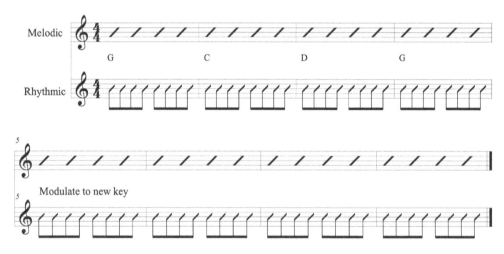

*Essential Elements for Developing an Improvisatorial Mindset*

## 1. Trust

If you are doing these exercises with others, I encourage you to trust the other members of your ensemble. Be open and receptive to any and all suggestions.

## 2. Ability to Listen

Some of these exercises will feel really fast, and you may think you do not have enough time to hear your own thoughts. I would encourage you to not only engage when you are a participant but also engage while you are outside of the participants. A great way to speed your reaction time is to have your brain actively engaged in the exercise throughout the whole class. Just because you may not be participating in a particular round shouldn't mean that you turn off your listening skills.

### 3. Synergy

A lot of these exercises help bring out synergy with the other members of your ensemble. The reflection exercise in particular will help you develop a synergy with another musician. Over the course of time, this synergy will translate to other more complicated musical experiences.

### 4. Micromanagement and Macromanagement

Thinking in the micro and macro level is a combination of being in the present and future simultaneously. However, it never exists in the past. Being in the moment involves focus, commitment, and cutting out distractions. Eliminating clutter from the head allows musicians the space to focus their energies on the present moment. The philosophy of intention to invention is a first step to help declutter the sight-reader's mind and transform it into an improviser's mind. As you go through these exercises, have a childlike sense of play and adventure. One of the best things about children playing, for example, is that they live in the moment. When young children play, they do not hyper-focus on whether something is right or wrong; rather, they focus on the fun. Should there be a mistake in the moment, let it go. You can always try again.

### 5. Realization and Stepping into the Deep

Some novice improvisers may not be accustomed to these types of exercises. For some, you may still feel apprehensive with these exercises. That is ok! Realize that even if you are apprehensive of what to play, you can always focus on the fun of exploring the music's character.

### 6. Confidence

In the Audience Input Exercise, if you are given the suggestion of "Play in Eb," you may feel like you do not know what to play. Remember that the suggestion was to "play in Eb," not play a fully improvised cadenza from a classical concerto, or bebop lines reminiscent of Dizzy Gillespie. Have the confidence that you can play an Eb scale, or repeating Eb notes, or an arpeggio articulated in a variety of ways. Anything that comes to mind that you can execute is considered a success.

### 7. Genuine Study of Craft and Practice

Over the course of time, as you listen and process more music in a particular genre, develop an improviser's mindset, and become comfortable with performing without preparing notes, the idea of creating something out of nothing will become easier.

### 8. Imagination

How can musicians know for certain if they are capable of improvisation? A great example to illustrate one's inherent capacity to improvise is a child's intrinsic use of imagination. During childhood, there are undoubtedly countless times where the craft of improvisation sharpens. A child hones their improvisational skills through play. For example, when a younger child may not have access to toys. When this occurs, he allows himself to improvise with materials that he may not initially intend as toys, for example, pots and pans as a drum set. You have the capability for an infinite number of ideas—give yourself permission to use your imagination.

36  *Establish an Improvisational Mindset*

At this point, musicians may be asking about how to execute intention within a variety of genres—such as performing Renaissance and Baroque period embellishments, Classical period cadenzas, jazz small group playing, and classical, contemporary chamber music. Before we can apply intention to a specific genre, novice improvisers should develop practical skills in molding coherent solos. So, how can novice players practice an improvised intelligible solo without being genre-specific? Are there exercises that can be explored and drilled to help them in this process?

The next chapters will explore how to utilize their newly formed improviser's mindset, take the mentally conceived musical idea, and shape it into a coherent solo. Subsequently, as they build a stronger improvisatorial foundation through a series of layered exercises, they can begin to construct a more compelling solo, which will eventually become more genre-specific. This step in my pedagogical approach to improvisation is to examine and develop a process I have called the *invention*.

# 4 Play What You Hear

## An Introduction to Invention

Intention, or the focus of learning *how* to improvise, can only take you so far. Intention is part of the learning process that involves 1) developing the ability to mentally create an idea, 2) manifesting essential elements within your mind to help in the creation process, and 3) utilizing exercises to help develop an improvisatorial nature. As musicians build stronger improvisatorial foundations through the series of layered exercises discussed in previous chapters, they will be ready for what comes next in the learning process.

In this section:

1. Focus on the instant translation of an idea from the mind to the instrument.
2. Work through music conversation exercises to help instantly translate ideas.
3. Exercise ways to create a better connection to your instrument.
4. Learn to embroider a melody and discover ways to improvise "between" notes.
5. Develop the ability to create your own coherent improvised solo.
6. Understand how to invent a compelling improvised solo.

The next part of the learning process in this book involves embroidering a pre-composed melody, then learning what to include in an entirely improvised solo, subsequently discovering what is needed to make the improvised solo compelling enough to become more genre-specific. The following chapters will examine my philosophies and pedagogical approach to discovering *what* to play and translating an idea into a musical reality. Thus, in the next section, my pedagogical approach to improvisation is to examine and develop a process I have called the *invention*.

It is not enough to focus our attention on developing a capacity to improvise. If that were true, then Harold Hill's famous "think system" would be a viable approach to playing an instrument. There needs to be a marriage between "how" to play with "what" to play. So, after completing a series of exercises to help instill an improvisatorial mindset, it is important to begin the process of focusing on *what* to improvise, or what I refer to as the *invention*. As stated in earlier chapters, "Mentally conceiving an idea is as straightforward as thinking about what needs to be said to another person." The trick then is to translate that idea into a reality instantly. So, how do you instantly translate an idea into a musical reality? Here is a fun exercise to help get you started:

**Musical Conversation Exercise**

Start with one note. Any note. The most comfortable note you can play. No time signature, no meter, no nothing—just one note. Think about what two friends would say to one another if they

DOI:10.4324/9781003341857-4

38   *Play What You Hear*

ran into each other, not seeing one another in a while. Think of that conversation and then play that conversation rhythmically on that one note.

> *Hello. How are you? It is so good to see you. How are Marge and the kids?*
> *I am well. It is really good to see you too. How long has it been? Marge and the kids are great.*

For example:

In the previous example, you will see meter, rhythm that matches mathematically to each bar, etc. This is only so you can have a visual of this exercise. Ideally, you should only think about the words in the conversation and play the words as you would say them to a person. There is no sense of time, pulse, meter, rhythm, etc . . . only your ability to translate the flow of the words through your nonverbal instrument. The idea is to eliminate all of the limitations that printed music and stylistically correct performance practices required of an improviser and only focus on the idea of translating a thought into music.

Try this several times with different conversations. I encourage you to try this exercise with other people, and then have a third person try to guess what you two were "talking" about.

Additionally, the more comfortable you become with this exercise, the more elements you can add. For example, slowly introduce meter to give yourself a pulse, key signatures to slowly add a harmonic twist to the conversation, or playing more than one note in stepwise motion to give your conversation a melodic element. In either case, always make sure that the words you are "saying" leads where you take the musical elements.

Here is another helpful technique to bring out the transition from intention to invention, developing a better connection with your instrument. Try this: Pick something accessible that you like, in this case: "Danny Boy."

Disclaimer: For the purpose of showing an example, this sheet music helps visually represent the discussion points. However, it is vital that when the learner is trying this technique, they do not write anything down or use any type of sheet music. This is all done by ear!

Melody: ***Memorize this Melody. Sing it. Then Play It the Way You Sing It***

Harmony: *Analyze and Internalize the Harmonies*

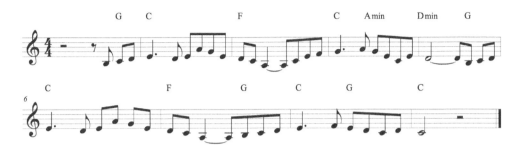

Sing the harmonies, then play the harmonies the way you sing it.

Rhythm: *Analyze and Internalize the Rhythm*

*Musical Nuance*

1) Listen to your favorite performance of this piece, or record someone that you respect playing it.
2) Memorize every nuance of the performance: Articulation, dynamics, phrasing, tempo, etc.
3) Sing every nuance.
4) Play it like you sing it.

Here is a list of 100 other easy, melodic, accessible songs to help with these exercises. Remember that the idea of these exercises is to do them by ear, and to practice the transition from intention to invention, developing a better connection with your instrument.

"A Whole New World" (Alan Menken)
"All I Ask of You" (Andrew Llyod Webber)
"All of Me" (Gerald Marks)
"All the Things You Are" (Jerome Kern)

40 *Play What You Hear*

"Almost Like Being In Love" (Frederick Loewe)
"Also Sprach Zarathustra" opening theme (Richard Strauss)
"Amazing Grace" (Traditional)
"Ashokan Farewell" (Jay Ungar)
"Autumn Leaves" (Johnny Mercer)
"Blue Monk" (Thelonius Monk)
"Blue Moon" (Richard Rogers)
"Bohemian Rhapsody"—Ballad Segment (Freddie Mercury)
"C Jam Blues" (Duke Ellington)
"Can You Feel the Love Tonight" (Elton John)
"Can't Help Falling in Love with You" (Jean Paul Egide Martini)
"Chariots of Fire" (Vangelis)
"Do-Re-Mi" (Richard Rogers)
"Don't Cry For Me Argentina" (Andrew Llyod Webber)
"Don't Get Around Much Anymore" (Duke Ellington)
"Easy Street" (Charles Strouse)
"Edelweiss" (Richard Rogers)
"Embraceable You" (George Gershwin)
"Fly Me to the Moon" (Bart Howard)
"For the Longest Time" (Billy Joel)
"Forrest Gump: Main Title" (Alan Silvestri)
"Freddie the Freeloader" (Miles Davis)
"Go the Distance" (Alan Menken)
"God Save the Queen" (Traditional)
"God Bless the Child" (Billie Holiday and Arthur Herzog Jr.)
"Greensleeves" (Traditional Christmas Carol)
"Habanera" (Georges Bizet)
"Hallelujah" (Leonard Cohen)
"Happy Birthday" (Traditional)
"Hark the Herald" (Christmas Carol)
"Harry Potter: Main Theme" (John Williams)
"Have Yourself a Merry Little Christmas" (Hugh Martin)
"Hello" (Lionel Richie)
"Hey Jude" (Paul McCartney)
"How High the Moon" (Morgan Lewis)
"I Don't Know How to Love Him" (Andrew Llyod Webber)
"I Fall In Love Too Easily" (Jule Styne)
"I Know Him So Well" (Benny Andersson and Bjorn Ulvaeus)
"I Will Always Love You" (Dolly Parton)
"I've Been Working on the Railroad" (Classic Children's Song)
"If I Only Had a Brain" (Harold Arlen)
"Imagine" (John Lennon)
"I've Never Been in Love Before" (Frank Loesser)
"Jingle Bells" (Christmas Carol)
"Joy to the World" (Christmas Carol)
"La donna e mobile" (Giuseppe Verdi)

"Let It Be" (Paul McCartney)
"Let It Go" (Robert Lopez and Kristen Anderson Lopez)
"Let It Snow, Let It Snow, Let It Snow" (Christmas Carol)
"Like Someone in Love" (Jimmy Van Heusen)
"Indiana Jones and the Raiders of the Lost Ark Main Theme" (John Williams)
"Jurassic Park Main Theme" (John Williams)
"The Godfather Main Theme" (Nino Rota)
"Mary Had a Little Lamb" (Classic Children's Song)
"Maybe" (Charles Strouse)
"Memory" (Andrew Llyod Webber)
"Misty" (Errol Garner)
"Moon River" (Henry Mancini)
"Mr. PC" (John Coltrane)
"Musetta's Waltz La Boheme" (Giacomo Puccini)
"My Favorite Things" (Richard Rogers)
"My Funny Valentine" (Richard Rogers)
"My Girl" (The Temptations)
"My Heart Will Go On" (James Horner)
"My Romance" (Richard Rogers)
"Night and Day" (Cole Porter)
"O Happy Day" (Traditional Gospel)
"O Holy Night" (Traditional Christmas Carol)
"O mio babbino" (Giacomo Puccini)
"O Sole Mio" (Eduardo di Capua and Alfredo Mazzucchi)
"Ode for the Birthday of Queen Anne" (George Frideric Handel)
"Oh, What a Night" (Bob Gaudio)
"Oh, What a Beautiful Mornin" (Richard Rogers)
"Over the Rainbow" (Harold Arlen)
"Piano Man" (Billy Joel)
"Pink Panther Theme" (Henry Mancini)
"Pomp and Circumstance Main Theme" (Edward Elgar)
"Queen of the Night Aria" (Wolfgang Amadeus Mozart)
"Rainbow Connection" (Paul Williams and Kenneth Ascher)
"Ride of the Valkyries Theme from Die Walkure" (Richard Wagner)
"Rocky Main Theme" (Bill Conti)
"Row, Row, Row Your Boat" (Classic Children's Song)
"Saint Thomas" (Traditional Bahamian Folksong)
"Santa Claus Is Coming to Town" (J. Fred Coots)
"Satin Doll" (Duke Ellington and Billy Strayhorn)
"Send in the Clowns" (Stephen Sondheim)
"Silent Night" (Traditional Christmas Carol)
"Simple Gifts" (Traditional)
"Someone Like You" (Adele and Dan Wilson)
"Someone to Watch Over Me" (George Gershwin)
"Sometimes I Feel Like a Motherless Child" (Traditional)
"Star Wars: Main Title" (John Williams)

42   *Play What You Hear*

"Suddenly Seymour" (Alan Menken)
"Summertime" (George Gershwin)
"Superman: Main Theme" (John Williams)
"Sweet Caroline" (Neil Diamond)
"That's Amore" (Harry Warren)
"The Christmas Song" (Traditional Christmas Carol)
"The Days and Wine of Roses" (Henry Mancini)
"The Flower Duet from Lakme" (Leo Delibes)
"The Prayer" (David Foster, Carole Bayer Sager, Alberto Testa, Tony Renis)
"The Sound of Silence" (Paul Simon)
"The Water Is Wide" (Traditional Scottish)
"The Way You Look Tonight" (Jerome Kern)
"Think of Me" (Andrew Llyod Webber)
"This Little Light of Mine" (Traditional Gospel)
"Tis the Last Rose of Summer" (Traditional Irish)
"Tomorrow" from the musical *Annie* (Charles Strouse)
"Toreador Song" (Georges Bizet)
"Twinkle, Twinkle, Little Star" (Classic Children's Song)
"Unchained Melody" (Alex North)
"Unforgettable" (Irving Gordon)
"We Are the Champions" (Freddie Mercury)
"Weekend in New England" (Randy Edelman)
"What a Wonderful World" (Bob Thiele and George David Weiss)
"When I Fall In Love" (Victor Young)
"When You Wish Upon a Star" (Leigh Harline)
"White Christmas from Holiday Inn" (Irving Berlin)
"Wishing You Were Somehow Here Again" (Andrew Llyod Webber)
"Yesterday" (Paul McCartney)
"You'll Never Walk Alone" from the musical *Carousel* (Richard Rogers)
Your country's national anthem

Throughout your studies, as you transition from hearing pre-written tunes to hearing your own musical ideas, you will understand that there is a myriad of methods to translate an idea into a musical reality. A strategy that I have found to be successful is to investigate the correlation between the composer, performer, and listener: the composer creates, the performer executes, and the listener reacts. An improviser must be all three, combining the actions of a composer, performer, and listener.

### Improviser as part-composer: *The Intended Creation*

Improvisation is real-time composition whereby the act of creating music occurs while it is performed. Hence, an improviser's thought process needs to mirror that of a composer in terms of translating an idea into a reality by developing a broader perspective on the piece's compositional construction. The part-composer improviser thinks about elements such as melodic contour, rhythmic variety, form, structure, tempo, dynamics, articulation, etc.

**Improviser as part-performer:** *The Invented Creation*

We categorize improvisation as what happens when a musician mentally conceives an idea and then simultaneously produces that sound in the moment—creating notes with harmonic density, rhythmic complexity, melodic emotion, etc. As a performer, the improviser must take the compositional elements and execute them in real time—conceiving how to execute and propel the piece forward simultaneously. The part-performer places meaning and adds depth to the musical elements of the improvisation. The part-performer thinks about the emotional content and the aesthetics of the music. The part-performer communicates ideas and adds an expressive significance to the complexities of the compositional elements.

**Improviser as part-listener:** *The Response to Creation*

Music is an experience that requires both someone who makes the music and someone who listens to it. The improviser's role is to listen intently, place value on the experience, and react to the surroundings, thus defining the piece as music. Without the improviser as part-listener, the piece could very well be considered noise and not music. Improvisers who listen will not only receive, they will take what is heard and react appropriately. The reaction is a critical piece of the improvisational puzzle and the most important aspect of the part-listener. The reaction of the part-listener is a natural consequence of listening. The listener part of improvising is critical to the music-making process, simply by the musician's ability to define and validate the sound as music. If done well, the response will propel the piece forward. As a response to what is heard, the part-listener will help drive the choices the part-composer makes, which, in turn, will drive how the part-performer chooses to express the material.

The relationship of the part-composer, part-performer, and part-listener is cyclic in nature. No one part is more important than the other, especially when learning to improvise. If at any point you should struggle with studying improvisation, ask yourself if you are in balance of all three parts. Perhaps you will need more focus on internalizing musical elements of a composition such as form, harmony, or melodic construction. On the other hand, perhaps the issue is a weakness in your ability to listen to your surroundings and react accordingly. Perhaps, its neither of those, and instead you need to dive deeper into what you are specifically trying to communicate and what feelings you are trying to convey. In either case, strive for balance.

Before musicians focus on a particular style, genre, or historical performance practice, they should contemplate the correlation between composer, performer, and listener and how that correlation could help translate an idea in real time. The contemplation and practice of how these three parts intersect is a vital step. Doing so will create an awareness of the music-making process from all sides. For someone who solely focuses on only one of the three parts, for example, the performer, without any awareness as a composer or listener—improvisation can be a daunting experience. These types of players may feel discouraged and overwhelmed and may question their capacity to improvise. Try not to get discouraged—take things one step at a time. Once you are comfortable, use the exercises in the following chapters to help bring out an inventive nature.

# 5 Embroider a Solo

Improvise Between Notes

This chapter's focus is about the process to embroider preexisting, already-composed, printed material. At first, this step may seem more reactive rather than creative because the musician responds to already composed melodies and identifies opportunities where notes can be added as embellishments. This reactive nature gives musicians the ability to recognize places in the music where improvised music could occur in the moment. Once a musician recognizes an opportunity to improvise, the creative mind is activated, thus paving the way to learn how to create a melody spontaneously.

Before a musician can fully be comfortable translating an original idea into a reality, an excellent transitional step is to embroider a solo—adding mentally conceived potential new notes and musical elements to a pre-composed melody. Understand that while an improvised solo is an opportunity for the soloist to express virtuosic skills, players do not need first to compose melodic figures from scratch. If creating a melody from the ground up is too much of a challenge in the early stages of development, try embroidering the main melodic ideas of a pre-composed piece. Use the composer's work as a tool or precursor to help begin creating solos from scratch.

When converting the composed themes into improvised ones, there are many possibilities to choose from, thus possible to "make it your own." Think of this list as the beginning stages of developing a vocabulary. Once there is an established vocabulary, improvisers can begin to think about how to construct their own solos. If we are learning *what* to play, are there any *what to play* options to help us decide where and when to use them? What follows is a series of options to learn and internalize in order to build a vocabulary of tools to use for the future. Disclaimer: The suggested use of each option is only a recommendation to help the developing improviser begin to learn the process of improvisation. The options (or ornaments) in this section mean to help an improviser start the process of creating their own improvised solo by embroidering a pre-composed melody and are not for the study of Baroque performance practice—it is meant as a learning tool to help a musician get started on the act of creating notes that are not printed.

**What to Play Options**

*1. Trill*

A trill is an interchange between two notes—a principal note and a secondary note.

Think of the creation of a trill as having three parts—the prep, the speed, and the ending. For the prep, begin to think about how to prepare the trill. Prepare the trill by placing the secondary note either a whole or half step above the primary note as determined by the key signature. For example, the secondary note above a trilled B in the key of A is a C#, whereas the secondary note above a trilled B in the key of G is a C natural. There are exceptions, especially considering various historically accurate performance practice rules; however, for the sake of this chapter, a good starting point would be to start the trill on the secondary note and elongate it. Here is an example:

Second, make sure that any option (trill, mordent, turn, etc.) matches the style of the original line. For example, a good starting place for a trill would be to match the speed of the trill with the tempo of the piece. If the piece is allegro, the pace of the trill should be fast. If the tempo of the piece is grave, then the speed of the trill should be slow and then speed up.

For example:

Last, think about how to end the trill. Try this: Add an anticipation when the resolution descends and a turn when the resolution ascends.

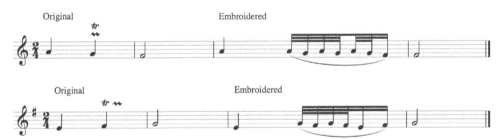

***Suggestion:*** Think about using trills at cadence points.

## *2. Turn*

I have always imagined a turn as being similar to the same action one would do when driving a motor vehicle. Imagine a driver attempting to maneuver between two cones. The driver may choose to turn left, then turn right, and then turn left again to avoid the cones, yet continuing down the same road. In music, think of a turn as maneuvering up and down instead of maneuvering left and right. A turn encompasses the primary note with a pair of notes—an upper and a lower note. Most of the time, it is accented on the beat or unaccented when performed between beats. When performing a turn between two beats, the turn's function becomes melodic. When performing a turn on the beat, the turn's function becomes harmonic.

See the subsequent illustration. In choice A, the turn is used as a melodic function decorating the original melodic line. In choice B, the turn is used as a way to alter the harmony while maintaining the integrity of the original musical line. An improviser needs to understand the two different functions to gain a robust vocabulary when creating in the moment.

*Suggestion:* Think about using turns when three ascending stepwise diatonic notes appear in succession.

### 3. Mordent

When trying to comprehend a mordent, ponder a situation that involves a dent in a car. Imagine a parked car in a grocery store parking lot suddenly hit by a rogue shopping cart. The act of impacting the car is quick, and the dent created in the car is comparatively small. A mordent is similar to the dent in that the added notes alter the main note like a dent would alter the car without redefining the definition of the car itself. Think of utilizing the mordent quickly, rhythmically, and with a small stepwise interval such as a half or whole step. Perform the mordent on the beat. In the subsequent example, the first C has a symbol above it that indicates adding an upper neighbor, whereas the second C has a symbol above it that indicates adding a lower neighbor.

*Suggestion:* Think about using mordents when a single quarter or perhaps a series of repeated quarter notes appear.

### 4. Appoggiatura

Another good way to embroider a melody is to consider creating suspension or tension and then resolving that dissonance. The tension is the new secondary note, and the resolution is the primary note. The resolution to a consonance from a dissonance can go in any direction. It can resolve downward or upward as long as the note is stressed, dissonant, and placed on the beat. Play these added notes on the beat. Hold them out for half the value of the primary note when the primary note can be divided by two. If the note is dotted, then the appoggiatura is held for two-thirds the value of the primary note. In this example, the performer must split the value of the half note—thus creating two equal quarter notes.

Applying the appoggiatura helps suspend the main melodic note by adding a new note before it and adopting a fixed relation to the length of the main note. Additionally, the appoggiatura should be stronger than the principal note: Think about adding more weight to the appoggiatura compared to the primary note.

*Suggestion:* Use appoggiaturas when there is an opportunity to create the most amount of tension. To begin, try focusing the use of appoggiaturas on longer valued notes such as half notes—doing so will help better develop an ear for how the harmony works in that particular piece.

## 5. Glissando

There are two types of glissando: Discrete and continuous. In either case, the use of glissando can be in fast or slow pieces. Discrete glissandi change pitch step by step, much like how a piano or harp player can only play certain centered pitches on the keyboard. For continuous glissandi, imagine a trombone player utilizing the slide to create a fun effect to the music. The trombone and other brass, woodwind, and string instruments can play notes in between centered pitches.

*Suggestion:* Think about using glissandi to fill in large leaps.

## 6. Neighbor Tones

A neighbor tone can be either a step higher or lower than the primary note. In this example, the improviser chose to add an upper neighbor E in between the fourth beat of the first bar and the first beat of the second bar, as well as adding a C# in between beat three and bear four in the second bar.

*Suggestion:* Find two of the same tones repeated consecutively in the melody, then add either an upper or a lower neighboring note.

## 7. Double Neighbor Tones

A double neighbor tone is similar to a neighbor tone in that it begins and ends on the same note. Yet, in this case, the improviser employs both an upper neighbor and a lower neighboring note. In this example, the improviser employs an upper neighbor (F) and immediately plays a lower neighbor (D) before playing the final E.

*Suggestion:* Like a neighbor tone, find two of the same tones repeated consecutively in the melody, but add both an upper neighbor and a lower neighbor note.

### 8. Passing Tone

Think of a passing tone as a way to connect two chord tones. In this example, the improviser added a quarter note D between E (the third of the chord) and C (the root).

*Suggestion:* Find a leap of a third; it could be between the root and the third, the third and the fifth, or any third and place a nonchord tone in between them.

### 9. Escape Tones

Think of an escape tone as an incomplete neighbor tone. In this example, the added F is up a half step from the primary tone, and then it is followed by a leap typically in the opposite direction of the preceding step. The added E is a step above the D, and then it is followed by a leap downward.

*Suggestion:* Find three descending stepwise notes and add escape notes between them.

### 10. Doubles

Take the melody and double each note. For example, if the primary note is a quarter note, add two eighth notes. If the primary note is eight notes, add two sixteenth notes, etc.

*Suggestion:* You can use doubles for most parts of a melody. I recommend starting the use of doubles on half, quarter, and eighth notes.

### 11. Fill the Space

Fill the space with a scale.

Fill the space with an arpeggio.

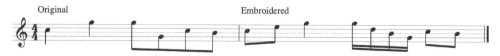

*Suggestion:* Seek out large intervals in the melody, and fill the space in between notes with either a scale pattern or an arpeggio.

## 12. Chord Tones

*Chord tone leap with a scale:*

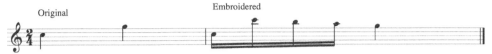

*Chord tone leap with an arpeggio:*

*Chord tone leap with a scale and an arpeggio:*

***Suggestion:*** Seek out large intervals and (1) leap to a chord tone and then play a scale, (2) leap to a chord tone and then arpeggiate, or (3) leap to a chord tone and then play a combination of a scale and arpeggio.

## 13. Nonchord Tones

*Nonchord leap with a scale:*

*Nonchord leap with an arpeggio:*

*Nonchord leap with a scale and an arpeggio:*

***Suggestion:*** Look for gaps between notes. Instead of only using chord tones to fill the gaps, add nonchord tones when embroidering a melody when there is an interval.

## 14. Change the rhythm

***Suggestion:*** Find any phrase and create rhythmic variation. For example, dotted figures are performed where straight eighth notes are written.

50  *Embroider a Solo*

**Embroider Exercise to Aid in Inventing Choices**

To be clear, this next exercise involves a piece of music without style, character, or phrasing. The purpose of the Embroider Exercise (and the following exercises in this chapter) is to cultivate a musician's ability to 1) recognize spots in the composition where improvised notes could be utilized and 2) create a new melody based on the pre-composed melody utilizing embellishments as a tool to learn the act of improvisation. It is not to teach how to use embellishments as it relates to a specific style, character, or phrase. Think of these exercises as an opportunity to learn to add new notes to a pre-composed melody and choose from a myriad of ornaments at a musician's disposal to create a new melody based on the pre-composed one.

*Embroider Exercise*

Utilize the original musical line in the subsequent figure, and embroider it using the options previously discussed in this chapter. Start by scanning the music, and look for opportunities to embroider the line. Make sure that there is a conscious effort to find places in this music where an appropriate option would logically be placed in this exercise. Do this exercise several times, each time choosing a different option and thus creating a "newly composed" piece each time.

In the example, I chose to begin by dividing the notes using a simple, rhythmic change. However, when I saw the same two notes (this time one is a half note, and the other is a whole note) in measures 14 and 15, I decided to fill the space with a D major scale connecting the low D half note to the high D an octave higher. Then, before playing the final higher octave D, I added an appoggiatura.

Now take a look at measures 5, 6, and 7. I noticed there is space between each of the quarter notes and that the notes in each measure outline a particular chord. Seeing this, I chose in measure 5 to fill the space with scale passages. In measure 6, I decided to fill the space with notes that outlined the chord, employing interval leaps. I continued to do so throughout the first half of measure 7 and then added a trill on the fourth beat. In measure 9, I detected that this measure is similar to measures 5 through 7. However, instead of embellishing the same way, I decided to add a glissando to each of those notes. Recall there is a myriad of choices when determining which option to use and that the improviser has the freedom to make the decisions in creating an embroidered line.

Regarding turns, I noticed a pattern in measures 8, 11, and 23. I became aware that in measure 8, the line started on the tonic and diatonically ascended to the third and that this pattern repeated in 11, with the exception of the rhythm. In 23, the pattern was the same, but the rhythm was the same as in measure 11. As a result, I chose in measure 8 to add a harmonic function turn, in measure 11 to add a melodic functioning turn, and in measure 23 to add a melodic functioning turn but on different notes to match the original notes in the measure.

As the piece progresses, so should the development of the improvised embellishments—doing this will help develop the improviser's own solos when he is ready to create one of his own. Make note (pun intended) of measures 16 and 17. In these measures, the solo is more than halfway complete. At this point, the development of the improvisation should become more complex. In measure 16 in particular, we observe a similar pattern of quarter notes outlining the chord. However, instead of doing the same thing earlier in the piece, I add more notes. I added notes that leap, scales, and arpeggios, followed by mordents in the next measure. I also added doubles on the eighth notes, creating new sixteenth notes in measure 18, neighboring notes in measure 20, and a multitude of notes incorporating leaps and scales in the penultimate measure.

### Other Sample Melodies to Embroider

Based on years of teaching and performing, I believe one of the best methods to improvise by adding notes to a composed piece is to internalize each option or ornament. Think of each ornament as vocabulary to use when speaking this musical language. These exercises are not merely about memorizing various ornaments. Instead, they are about developing an internalized dictionary of musical ideas to draw upon when searching for the right "word" to use on command. The deeply rooted ornaments will free up the improviser's mind to focus more on the color of the line and find opportunities to embellish instead of struggling with how to play the ornament physically. Improvisers can conquer the struggle with how to embroider a piece if they drill the various options in different keys every day until it becomes automatic and without physical effort. Once the options are learned, the improviser can then focus more on the character of the piece. The ultimate goal for this stage in improvisational development is discovering which options will best serve the piece.

For the following musical examples, utilize the original line and embroider it using the options previously discussed. Start by scanning the music, and look for opportunities to embroider the line. Make certain that there is a conscious effort to find places where an appropriate ornament could be utilizied. Do this exercise several times, each time making different choices and thus creating "newly composed" pieces.

Embroider these melodies:

*Embroider Exercise Melody #1*

*Embroider Exercise Melody #2*

*Embroider Exercise Melody #3*

*Embroider Exercise Melody #4*

*Embroider Exercise Melody #5*

54    *Embroider a Solo*

**Advanced Exercise:**

> Record yourself improvising a melody. Play the recording of yourself back, and transcribe it on manuscript paper. Then look at the transcription for opportunities to embellish and add ornaments based on the original musical line. Without writing anything down, take the original melody you created and recorded, play the recording back, and finally, play along with the recording, embellishing as you play.

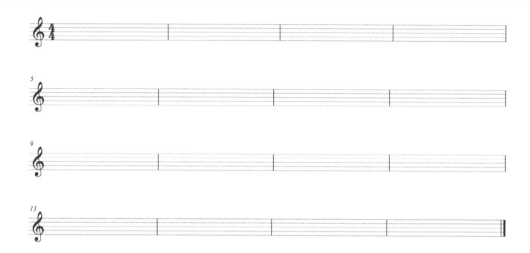

*The Essential Elements Applied to Embroidering the Original Line*

### 1. Trust

Trust that with thoughtful, focused preparation, the notes will come when they are needed. Trust that over time, you will be able to recognize opportunities to add to the melody.

### 2. Ability to Listen

When looking at the pre-composed melody, listen to how the melody sounds mentally before attempting to embroider. The melody will provide the harmonic and rhythmic elements needed to embellish the melodic line. Also, feel free to add various other musical elements such as improvised articulation, dynamics, and different musical nuances to the pre-composed piece.

### 3. Synergy

Synergize all three parts of improvisation: 1) improvisation from the perspective of a performer, 2) improvisation from the perspective of a composer, and 3) improvisation from the perspective of a listener.

### 4. Micromanagement and Macromanagement

Think in terms of both the micro and macro level. The improviser should have developed a strong vocabulary of ornaments and can recognize opportunities to use them while at the same time understand the direction of the whole piece and what it is trying to convey. Thinking simultaneously at the micro and macro levels will assist the improviser in seeing the entire picture while instantaneously hearing what color to add to the figurative painting.

## 5. Realization

Realize that the objective is to develop tools to use to embellish the original musical line. It is a helpful precursor to creating your own solo. Realize that the creativity involved at this stage is not so much generating something out of nothing; instead, it is inventing an enhancement to what is already written, thus creating something completely new and different. Improvisers must also recognize, in the moment, the opportunity to embellish when it arises and which tool matches the opportunity. What also helps direct the performer to make informed improvisational decisions is when she realizes the musical nuances of the original line. If the improviser always places musicality above all the other elements, then she will be a much more effective improvising artist.

## 6. Stepping into the Deep

An improviser should step into the deep and ensure that she is not falling into the same patterns. She should record herself to make sure that she is utilizing a variety of ornaments. It is important that she uses various ornaments as she progresses, not just the comfortable ones.

## 7. Confidence

Strive to demonstrate confidence in every performance. Should there be a circumstance of doubt, the improviser should allow the ear to lead the way. She should have confidence that the ear (ability to hear the harmony, rhythmic drive, and melodic contour) will take her in the right direction. With the ear leading the way, coupled with an integration of ornaments into her musical vocabulary, she will perform the right ornament at the right time. If she finds herself making mistakes in the moment of execution, she should be confident that she will make the proper adjustment.

## 8. Genuine Study of the Craft

The thing about adding notes to a pre-composed melody is that it may take time to develop the ability to make faster choices in the moment. Taking the time to study the pre-composed melody will help develop the ability to make quick note choices in the moment.

## 9. Practice

When provided with a blank slate to improvise, the challenge for most beginners is not typically knowing what to play but having too many artistic choices without realizing how to use the various options. To begin, practice one ornament at a time. This will result in a breakdown of the beginner's barrier, thus creating a comfortable environment for improvisation. The more she practices in this way, the better she will become at generating ideas on the spot.

## 10. Imagination

The use of imagination has helped me master the art of embroidering a pre-composed melody. Play through the melody examples again, and imagine what that melody could represent. For example, play melody example number 4, and imagine that it represents a tree throughout the four seasons. Imagine the various directions of tree branches in the spring. As you move through summer, imagine how tall and wide the tree is blowing through the wind. Then fall comes, and the leaves are different colors. Can you see those images in your head? What are the sounds of those images? The winter comes, and the tree lies dormant. Finally, toward the end, there is a return to spring. What would those images sound like to you?

Once you are comfortable with embellishing a pre-composed melody, begin to create your own melodies. The following two chapters answer the questions: What do musicians need in order to create a solo? How do they begin the process of creating one from scratch? They could start to address the process in one of two ways—and preferably both: By displaying technical prowess on the instrument and also by expressing a sentiment through the instrument, musically, emotionally, or spiritually. Both are tall orders, but it is possible to create a solo with the proper guidelines. The next chapter discusses five specific steps.

# 6 Construct a Solo

## Compose in Real Time

What do soloists new to improvisation need in order to create a solo? How do they begin the process of creating one without feeling overwhelmed? Based on my experience performing improvisation throughout my career, I believe these questions could be answered in one of two ways, preferably both: By displaying technical prowess on the instrument and expressing something musically, emotionally, or spiritually through the instrument. This is a tall order, but it is possible to create a solo with the proper guidelines. For this chapter, the purpose is to train musicians to learn to improvise a solo a cappella. Here are five specific steps to follow, with detailed subsequent explanations:

1. Explore melody.
2. Discover harmony.
3. Understand form.
4. Internalize the nuance.
5. Know that imagination is limited to what technique allows.

### 1. Explore Melody

Improvising melodies involves creating compositionally sound themes that match the intent and style of the piece. Here are some thoughts to consider when improvising melodies, along with exercises to implement:

A. *Melodies should be simple enough to make a point clear, consisting of smaller melodic motifs.*

**Exercise:** Begin by hearing a short, simple melody in your head. Try to hear all aspects of your melody. The more detailed, the better. Listen for the tempo, the rhythm, the specific notes in your melody, dynamics, etc. Consider this, are you able to sing it back to yourself? Or a more important question would be, If someone were to hear you sing this melody, would they be able to sing it back to you? If the answer is "yes," you are on the right track. If the answer is "no," then go back and think of something simpler (involving fewer notes and uncomplicated rhythms). The idea is to create a simple melody so that a listener could quickly understand it and easily relay it back.

**Example:**

DOI:10.4324/9781003341857-6

Still having problems hearing a melody? Try incorporating these parameters:

B. *Use notes in a stepwise motion.*

**Exercise:** Start your improvisation on any note you desire. Allow yourself only to move in a stepwise motion from one note to the next. In this exercise, your entire improvisation will be melodies with preceding notes and notes leading to the following note with the interval no greater than a major second. Here again, keep the melodies short and simple.

**Example:**

C. *Start each phrase on a different chord tone, avoiding using the same note that started the phrase.*

**Exercise:** With every phrase utilizing a stepwise motion, the next step is directing your attention to the harmonic elements of the melody. Begin each phrase on a different chord tone, and focus your energy toward hearing how a phrase would end and how that phrase could lead to another one. The idea is to stay reasonably close to the tonic key, emphasizing chord tones at the beginning and end of phrases.

D. *Develop melody.*

**Exercise:** When comfortable with creating melodies, avoid repeating the melodic passage. Instead, create different melodies and attempt to connect each one together. If the intent is to create a sequence, then repeating is fine. However, repeating yourself musically is generally akin to listening to a guest speaker constantly repeat his thesis statement; at some point, the audience wants to hear how the topic develops.

Main melody

Developed: By condensing

Developed: By elongating

Developed: By fragmentation

Developed: By embroidering

## 2. Discover Harmony: Describing Harmonic Elements of Good Solos

Once there is competency in creating a melody, move on to mastering the next element—discovering harmony. Consider the following when focusing energy on the harmony:

A. *Intervals need to be resolved.*

> **Exercise:** Begin by playing the chord on piano and singing the outline of each chord as written. Then try it again, only this time don't play the piano, just sing the written exercise. Then finally, play the written arpeggios on your instrument, or if possible, sing and play the arpeggios at the same time. Drop or raise octave as appropriate.

As you become better at hearing the outline chordal structure, I would encourage you to begin on the third and resolve down to the fifth instead of starting on the root note. Here again, sing first and then play it on your instrument.

Or beginning on the fifth and resolving down to the seventh. Remember to sing first, then play it on your instrument!

Now try this all again without looking at the written arpeggios.

B. *Utilize chord progressions with common tone chords.*

**Exercise:** Begin by playing the chord on piano, and sing the outline of each chord as written. Then try it again, only this time don't play the piano, just sing the written exercise. Then finally, play the line on your instrument, or, if possible, sing and play the line at the same time.
To be clear, this musical line is only an example for the reader to use as a learning tool. The goal is to practice this exercise by ear. Notice how the four chords all have common tones, for example, the F chord in the second measure shares a common note of C with the preceding measure (measure 1) and an A with the following measure (measure 3). In this exercise, as

you play in measure one, look ahead to the second measure and find a note that both chords share. Then play that common tone on the downbeat of the measure. Do this for the ensuing measures.

See example:

**Now try it in these keys:**

C. *Use the augmented fourth—this pitch is a leading tone to the dominant.*

**Exercise:** The purpose of the exercise is to learn how to use the augmented fourth to lead to the dominant. Notice how you outline some form of the major arpeggio in the first three beats and then play the augmented fourth leading to the root of the dominant.
Begin by playing the chord on piano, and sing the outline of each chord as written. Then try it again, only this time don't play the piano, just sing the written exercise. Then finally, play this exercise on your instrument, or, if possible, sing and play the line at the same time.

D. *Explore chromaticism but reaffirm the home tonality at the end.*

**Exercise:** It is helpful to have another person accompany you for this exercise. If another person is available, have them repeat consistent Cmaj7 chords. If another person is not available, there are plenty of online resources that can accompany you with repeating Cmaj7 chords. As the repeated Cmaj7 chords continuously play, incorporate chromaticism. Using the subsequent example, begin by playing an outline of a C# maj chord and then resolve it by playing a C maj chord. Then in the third bar, play the outline of a B maj chord and then resolve to a C maj chord. Next, try to incorporate some of these discordant notes while improvising simple melodies. Just make sure that after you include a "wrong" note, to resolve that tension by playing a note that fits in the chord. One of the goals of this exercise is to 1) become comfortable with the discordant sound and 2) play with the idea of harmonic tension and release.

E. *Melodies should drive toward an end.*

A critical element I have discovered on stage performing improvisation is mastering the art of being in the moment. For instrumentalists, it is ensuring and then trusting that one's theoretical, technical, and musical skills are solidified to utilize the elements of music that propel the piece forward. Having a solid foundation will help clear the mind to better be in the moment, whether in rehearsal or concert. I have found that when the mind is clear, there is room to create solos that drive toward a logical end and affect how the entire piece comes to an end.

**Exercise**: Anything you say needs to have a purpose musically. It is not enough to play a melody. Make certain that your melodies are driving to an end of a phrase with specific harmonic purpose. Mentally conceptualize the sound of the harmonic progression presented below. Sing this I- IV-ii-V-I chord progression in a key of your choosing and then play it on your instrument. Next, as you practice improvising melodies that drive forward, try to incorporate the encircled notes. These notes will help you connect the chord changes and harmonically propel your melody.

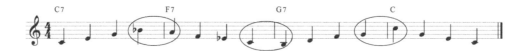

## 3. Understanding the Form

Finally, when novice improvisers have a grasp on the preceding elements, I suggest to them that they should progress to understanding the form of a solo. Novice improvisers can determine the form of an improvised solo by answering the question: How can I create an introduction or opening statement that modulates or transitions to a developed middle section and comes back to the ending tonic? Easy, right?

This may sound complicated, but let us break it down. For right now, let's not worry about playing over a particular set of chord progressions or in a particular style. Right now, just play an opening improvised statement or main melody. Keep it simple, short, and singable. For example:

Then over the next four bars, implement a few of the choices from Chapter 5, "Embroider a Solo."

Finally, come back in the last four measures by restating your main melody:

You did it! You created a melody that is understandable, you altered that melody, and then you returned to the theme. At first, try not to veer too far from the tonic key, keep melodies short and simple, and improvise in short two- or four-bar phrases. I have constantly reminded students over the years that once they are comfortable with combining melody, harmony, rhythm, and form, then—and only then—they can expand into more extended, more complicated solos.

## 4. Internalize the Nuances

One of the best ways to internalize the nuances of a piece is to listen to music composed by that composer—and not just the music he wrote for one particular instrument. By listening to all of the music composed by the composer—from his early period to his last piece—improvisers will get a sense of the compositional style, who he was as a musician, and an overall sense of the musical choices that would emulate the composer. Another suggestion to adopt a composer's style is to transcribe his thematic material of works. For example, if you improvise a cadenza within a concerto by Haydn, listen to his "Symphony No. 94," second movement, and transcribe the main "Surprise" melody. If performing a piece by Miles Davis, listen to "Freddie Freeloader" (*Kind of Blue*), and transcribe the main themes.

## 5. Know that Imagination Is Limited to What Technique Allows

Part of improvising involves executing the perfect balance between technique and imagination. Too much technique with little imagination will make for a boring improvisation that does not tell a very good story. On the flip side, too much imagination and not enough technique will put the improviser in a position of having a plethora of ideas without the technical fundamentals to execute them.

Think of technique as the tool a sculptor uses to carve out her work. The technique is only a means to an end. If musicians practice and sharpen the technical tools, they will have an easier time creating the improvisations they imagine. Ensure you have enough facility on your instrument to

- project fundamentals of music theory including the construction of intervals, scales, chords, and chord progressions,
- be effortless in your major and minor scales and arpeggios,
- be fluent in major, minor, and dominant chords,
- have a good sound, and execute a variety of types of articulation,
- navigate the different ranges at various dynamic levels

**Improvisation construction:** Understand the parameters regarding melody, harmony, meter, rhythm, style, articulation, phrasing, length, and form. Our melodic, harmonic, and structural choices seem endless with today's modern ear and worldwide resources. With so many choices now at our disposal, why limit ourselves to just practicing one aspect at a time? For a good reason! Practice one element at a time and then slowly start to combine them. Work on exploring melodies, then improve those melodies by discovering the addition of connecting to harmony, then add a sense of structure by understanding form. It is much easier for me to begin the process of learning to improvise once I eliminate my choices. Eliminating choices allows the performer to focus on one thing at a time, slowly building their arsenal of weapons of mass creation.

### The Essential Elements Applied When Constructing a Solo

### 1. Trust

For improvised melodies to come out naturally and in the moment, I must *trust* that my theoretical, technical, and musical skills are strong enough for the imagination to draw at will the musical element it needs. Focus on creating a simple melody and developing it, then trust that it will create a path that leads to a cohesive, clear musical message.

### 2. Ability to Listen

I have discovered in the practice room that another effective strategy to improvise a solo is to imagine myself as being an extension of the composer. A successful way to accomplish this is to *listen* to all the music by that composer. Transcribing the main melodies of various pieces written by the composer and then analyzing the construction of those melodies will take the improviser one step closer to emulating a stylistically correct improvisation.

### 3. Synergy

Remember that a way to better understand the construction and implementation of a solo is to consider yourself a partner with the piece's composer. I work to *synergize* the information presented in the written material in the practice room, that is, chord changes, stylistic performance approaches regarding articulation and phrasing, main melodic contour, etc. Using the written material and understanding the culture, time period, and compositional tendencies as musical nourishment will fuel the improviser's own improvised material.

## 4. Micro and Macro Points of View

Not only do I think of myself as a partner to the piece's composer, but I must also think like the composer—especially when creating in the moment. Composers have *micro and macro* views when creating a composition: They consider how the smaller phrases connect to the overall arch of the aural story. An improviser must employ the same micro and macro view when creating on the spot. When I assist students in analyzing their improvised solos, I remind them that they need to consider the micro/macro connection instantaneously. They need to understand how the smaller parts of their improvisations (the note choices, rhythmic choices, smaller phrases) connect with how the overall harmonic progression, rhythmic drive, and melodic contour shape the entire improvised solo.

## 5. Realization

I constantly reflect on the objective of the solo. My teacher Earl Carter helped me *realize* that to say something of value in the moment, one needs to have a clear goal. Mr. Carter helped me early on in my studies with self reflection, to consider and ask myself (and answer) questions such as What kind of sound do I want to create? What is the larger goal of my solo? What smaller goals can I achieve along the path to accomplishing the larger goal? How can I best represent the composer while incorporating my sense of musicality? A well-defined intention instills a sense of purpose in the improviser. This purpose (or goal) will direct how he makes musical choices in the moment. When musicians have small isolated practice goals, they will have the tools to answer the more significant, more artistic questions.

## 6. Stepping into the Deep

I have often found myself at risk of becoming complacent with what I create. I must remind myself to *step into the deep* and venture outside of my comfort zone to combat this problem. To avoid complacency, I contemplate how to drive a piece forward by using various harmonies with dominant functions. I like to use alternative chords such as the supertonic, subdominant, and submediant instead of secondary dominants and tonic chords. Additionally, I might consider using the parallel minor or submediant chord as a substitute for the I chord. In a nutshell, the moment an improviser is comfortable utilizing elements to construct the improvised solo is when he should expand by utilizing the wealth of compositional resources available.

## 7. Confidence

The first time I heard the likes of Maynard Ferguson, Jon Faddis, Ellis Marsalis, Tito Puente, and countless others live in concert, I knew that the best improvisers are those who exude a level of *confidence* that is assertive, secure, and unbreakable. Later in my career as a performer and educator, I discovered that confidence could develop out of a high standard of preparation and understanding of the compositional style, historical and cultural background, theoretical and compositional techniques, and knowledge of the mechanics of the instrument. These elements provide a treasure map where the performer mentally conceives the sound and then allows the sound to develop over time naturally.

## 8. Genuine Study of the Craft

Eventually, you will need to analyze how master improvisations construct their solo. There are plenty of books published on this subject. When you are ready, seek out these resources and take the next steps to study, internalize, and memorize the masters. But only when you are ready. In the meantime, listen to recordings, or better yet, go to concerts with improvisation and soak in the wealth of education one could glean from such performances.

## 9. Practice

As stated earlier in this book, my definition of music is an instance in time when a listener places value on an experience created by a composer. Music, in my view, must have one or more of the following three elements: A composer, a listener, and a performer. However, when improvising, one must incorporate each of these three key ingredients into a blended mixture. An improviser must be one-third listener, one-third composer, and one-third performer simultaneously. Practice and study all three perspectives slowly. Take your time. There is no need to rush the learning process.

## 10. Imagination

Edward Hopper said, "No amount of skillful invention can replace the essential element of imagination." As you become comfortable with the nuts and bolts of creating an improvised solo, go back and use some of the imagination etudes. For example, use imagination etude 2: Tell a story. In this etude, use your imagination and create a short story. The story should have a beginning, middle, and end. Then imagine the sound of the short story's soundtrack. However, make sure that you are implementing a combination of the musical elements discussed in this chapter that will aid in expressing the sound and direction of the story.

Once performers are comfortable with creating an improvised melody, they need to understand the significance of producing a more meaningful, compelling solo. This is achieved by, among other aspects, incorporating the concept of a phrase. The next chapter helps the reader understand the definition of a phrase and how to incorporate it into a particular form as a soloist and within a group setting. The chapter includes a step-by-step procedure to understand phrases related to improvisation, groove, and aesthetic. The introduction of a number of aesthetic exercises help bring out the creative side of a solo and helpful ideas for getting out of creative slumps.

# 7 Cultivate Creativity

## Improvise Compelling Notes

Improvisers who desire to improve their real-time compositional skills should try focusing their energies on playing in phrases. In addition to learning how to draw in an audience by creating a solo's actual notes, they must learn how to shape those notes to express an idea, opinion, or emotion. When improvisers try to express something significant to another person, they must understand that it is challenging to say everything that needs to be said all at once. Therefore, there must be some time given to the other person to process the information received. Subsequently, as an improviser, one must create statements that express the most important point, allowing it to connect to the next statement, and so on until the improviser completes enough phrases to express the story she is trying to tell.

This brings us to the question What is a phrase? The most common definition of a phrase is a series of notes that express a concept. The creation of a phrase within the context of a larger work with multiple players involved can be a challenge. This chapter will assist with the process of transmitting an invented solo into a compelling solo. It will also discuss how a phrase is created when improvisers understand and implement their role within an ensemble. Whether that role is as a sideman within an ensemble or as a featured soloist, an improviser's challenge is to create something that conveys an idea in a meaningful way.

So, what makes an improvised solo compelling? Throughout my career as a performing musician and educator, I have discovered that the answer can be narrowed down to three areas—inventiveness, groove, and aesthetic.

### Inventiveness Is Freedom

Improvisation in an ensemble gives players the freedom to express themselves. Improvisers see a lead sheet, in the case of a jazz musician, or the main theme of a Baroque dance, in the case of a Baroque musician, as a blank canvas to paint a musical picture using endless amounts of colors but remaining within the canvas. Each musician in an ensemble has the freedom to choose the painted colors (i.e., note choices, phrase length, articulation, etc.) when soloing. In addition, and perhaps more importantly, they should understand their role and improvise in accordance to that role as it relates to the other members of the band. Studying and practicing to a point where an improviser is free from any limitations of technique achieves this aspect of performance.

### Groove Is a Form of Negotiation

Groove is a matter of coordination and balance and teaches the musician how to be diplomatic. Yes, an improvising musician has freedom, but the other musicians in an improvisational ensemble

DOI:10.4324/9781003341857-7

70　*Cultivate Creativity*

also have the same freedom. If every musician has the freedom to create, there must be a way to equalize each improvisation so chaos does not ensue. Groove is an approach to the rhythm and a shared responsibility that all improvisers must be cognizant of when playing together. They must work together in tandem to bring out the best in each other's improvisation. You will achieve groove when you listen to each other and synergize the strengths and contributions of each musician, working as a team for the desired result.

## Aesthetic Is the Critical Component

Improvising with others requires *inventiveness* and *groove*, yet one must consider the aesthetic aspect. Think of aesthetic as an artistic perspective that expresses the depth of humanity buried within the core of an improviser's soul. An improvising musician must dig deep within himself and discover what needs to be said in the moment in such a way that it is in balance with his inventive choices and the way he interprets the rhythm. The freedom to make inventive choices and creating a groove with other musicians are secondary to the aesthetic goal of expressing and maintaining musical integrity.

All three elements must be incorporated when learning how to create a compelling improvised solo, both as a soloist and with others. Improvisation is more than just what notes to play over what chord. It is about comprehending *how* to communicate and *what* to use to best express an emotion in the moment. It considers one's role and how to express lines that support or lead a musical thought. And finally, it is a coming together of different musical perspectives to create a better artistic product.

## Inventiveness

How does an improviser invent a phrase? Where does a spontaneous musical phrase come from? According to Mr. Carter, "It depends on the type of conversation and what you choose to contribute." Each improviser in an ensemble has an equal say in the musical exchange. They each come to the table prepared to engage in meaningful conversation. Improvisers do this by preparing the knowledge (i.e., mastering one's instrument, understanding form and harmony, performing in the correct style, transmitting any idea they can think of through their instrument, etc.) needed to be a competent conversationalist. They prepare themselves so that they have what they need when a musical moment happens, necessitating an interjection into the conversation. There are many roles within an improvisational ensemble, such as single-note players, harmonic-based players, and rhythmically based players.

Single-note players are improvisers who typically perform no more than one note at any given time, such as trumpet, saxophone, and trombone, compared to improvisers who play instruments that are capable of playing more than one note at a time, such as piano and guitar. Notice when listening to hard-bop musicians such as Clifford Brown and Sonny Rollins, their solos sound like a multitude of eighth notes rattled off, firing them out almost seemingly without taking a breath. Playing long phrases as these artists do is challenging yet rewarding. Advanced strategies employed to sound like these musicians involve

1. articulating every note,
2. adding harmonic substitution,
3. creating resolution between chord tones,
4. incorporating rhythmic variety,

5. delaying the resolution or anticipating the resolution of the next chord before it arrives, and
6. chromatically approaching notes to extend the phrase.

It is natural for a beginning improviser to want to play long phrases. However, most developing improvisers do not have the experience to employ these tactics necessary for pulling it off. In addition to their lack of experience, some developing improvisers play long phrases because they

1. struggle with finding the idea of their solo,
2. are not being proactive and confident with their intention, and
3. have a hard time hearing the chord changes and get lost.

For the novice improviser, start with short two- or four-bar phrases. The more advanced one becomes, the longer a phrase can be. Fundamentally, there is nothing wrong with playing long phrases. Yet we must keep in mind the intention to invention process. Focus your mind on what to express rather than becoming attached to playing a lot of notes.

Here is an example of a phrase that is long.

In the previous example, there is a ten-bar phrase without any space in it. For the novice, this musical phrase is too long and similar to a run-on sentence in grammar. A first step in creating confident lines would be to create small phrases, allowing the phrase to breathe by creating two-bar phrases instead of one large one. Make a statement with the line, and do not create run-on sentences. It would be better to have consistent two-bar phrases or four-bar phrases as opposed to the whole chorus being one phrase, ten bars long. For example, here is the same long phrase adjusted to a short phrase version: Try breaking it up as stated in the next example and play it again. See if you can hear the difference between a solo that is essentially one phrase as opposed to many different phrases.

In this example, phrases are smaller in order for the idea to breathe. Beginning improvisers should play shorter phrases because it will

1. force them to be intentional in what they want to project,
2. provide time for them to think about what to play next, and
3. instill an awareness of the supporting harmony.

Here is an example of a solo that utilizes two-bar phrases:

Shorter phrases will help a listener easily understand the conveyed message. With shortened phrases, the solo will have clear, concise, and simple statements for people to understand. If the listener happens to be a fellow performing musician, then clear, shorter phrases will aid in how they contribute their portion to the piece. As improvisers master shorter phrases, they can begin the process of combining shorter phrases, creating longer phrases that cross bar lines. Remember that creating a musical line is to develop distinctive, well-crafted phrases throughout the entire solo. These lines should transcend the chord-scale relationship and express something that lives deep within the improviser's soul. Achieve this by practicing slowly, thriving to internalize the harmonic progression.

## Groove

A proven way to learn groove is to construct phrases within an improvisational ensemble working with other people. The ideal situation is that any given improviser knows enough of the subject area that he can contribute something unique based on his own experiences and his own musical role. Each contribution should amalgamate into a new musical concept that cannot be possible without the other musicians involved. When musicians get together, their goal is to have an engaging, intelligent musical conversation with one another. The primary role of each musician is to provide (within the context of their instrument) substance for that conversation. At different points in that conversation, each person will be taking the lead of that conversation. For example, how would an ensemble that consists of a drummer, bass player, and pianist exhibit groove?

### *Role of the Drummer*

How does the drummer take the lead? What is her responsibility or role? The drummer is responsible for the rhythmic language of the conversation. A central aspect of improvisation is the rhythmic value of the piece. Given the nature of percussion instruments, one can surmise the drummer leads the way in setting up the other players to contribute to the rhythmic language of the piece of music. It is important to note that regardless of an improviser's primary function, they all have to be fluent in the rhythmic language to participate fully in the conversation.

### *Role of the Piano Player*

How does the piano player take the lead? What is his responsibility or role? The piano player provides the color of the piece. He decides the texture and fills the space with a variety of harmonic choices. After rhythm, the next most important aspect is the harmony. The piano will take the lead with the harmony. He supports the melody, adds harmonic value to the rhythm, and creates the space needed to define the harmonic qualities of the piece.

### *Role of the Bass Player*

How does the bass player take the lead? What is his responsibility or role? The bass player takes the lead on the outline of the chords. He provides an outline of the chords, creating a foundation upon which the piano player can lay his harmonic head.

Roles can change. Nothing in the rules suggests that a drummer must always play time and never the melody, or a trumpet player must play the main theme and never the bass line. The goal is to have a group mind in determining the purpose of the piece, how it will ultimately end, and which musician will take on which role.

Whether an improviser plays the role of a pianist, bass player, drummer, or a single note player, in general, the function of an improvising musician is to believe in the infinite influence of integration. I understand that as an individual, no one person has a complete set of proficiencies. I've learned to recognize that the more improvising musicians can come together around a piece of music, the greater the art becomes. If you want to learn to improvise in compelling ways, you must accept and embrace the uniqueness of other artists.

A great way to make an improvised solo compelling, creative, and innovative, especially when playing with others, is to think of yourself as similar to being a diplomat in a foreign country. Diplomats want what is in the best interest of their respective countries. At the same time, there must be a willingness to give up something in order to receive something more remarkable in the end, a sort of compromise of give and take. As a musical diplomat, your preparation should only be a starting point to bring something to the table. Improvisers should be open enough to accept different ideas that culminate in a new expression of a piece. For example, the drummer may bring his own unique perspective to the piece. This different perspective could inspire the sax player to try something new with the melody.

## Aesthetic

Once the notes of an invented phrase groove with other musicians, how then does one shape the notes to express an opinion? How does one construct a creative musical line that tells a story in an improvised form such as a fake tune? It is simple—listen to how others do it and copy them, at least at first. Mr. Carter once told me, "If you have ever listened to a piece of music and felt something, then you can create an aesthetic quality to the note you are playing."

I have long considered listening as the primary way, in which a musician begins the creative process. To help bring about an aesthetic quality to your improvisation, listen to the emotional thoughts connected to the improvised piece. Try to focus your energy on remembering a certain connected feeling and then transmit that feeling through your instrument. Allow the notes to be a servant to the intended emotion.

Someone who improvises notes does not merely follow instructions, such as the chord/scale relationship. Instead, an improviser thinks about what to express and how to best express those ideas or emotions through her instrument in the moment. Improvisers look for nuance, for a color shift, striving for the next change in the musical atmosphere. Therefore, an improviser who desires to improve must understand that it is not only about the improvised notes within the phrase; it is about creating different characters to communicate an idea. The question that remains then is how to accomplish this. Anyone who has ever taught or studied this would say that it is one of the hardest things to teach and one of the hardest things to learn. The act of learning how to truly phrase a feeling is something that will develop over a lifetime, takes a lot of practice, and takes a lot of experience performing with exceptional musicians. However, I have found success in developing a series of aesthetic exercises to help developing improvisers cultivate an aesthetic quality to their solos.

### Aesthetic Exercises

#### Aesthetic Exercise Step 1: Listen

Since listening is the primary source of applying aesthetic qualities to the phrase, it is important to practice listening. When you listen to music, you are studying interpretation. Once you understand how to interpret, you can apply it to your own playing. Take a score, whether it be orchestral, pop, rock, jazz, or any other style of music, and follow along, reading the part while you listen so you know what you are interpreting. A chord symbol is just a symbol that represents what notes to play until you hear how someone interprets it to express a feeling. So, a beginning step in developing your aesthetic sensibility is to listen with purpose, following along with a score or transcription, if possible, so that you can educate yourself on how to interpret improvised notes into an expressive thought. Better yet, engage in a call-and-response exercise with a professional improviser, copying their style and nuance to each called phrase.

#### Aesthetic Exercise Step 2: Experiment

Once you have taken the time to listen to an extraordinary amount of music in the improvisational style of your choice, then the next step is to experiment. You must be intentional when discovering the different colors of the sound within any given phrase over the course of the entire piece. Experiment with expressing ideas and emotions through the sound. When you were listening to the piece you are trying to improvise, you should have been listening for the piece's character.

Now it is time to try to capture that character in your playing. As you are practicing this, ask yourself, *Is that all of the ideas that I want to project in this piece?* rather than *Have I played enough notes in this phrase?* There is more you can say in one sustained note than if you played a hundred notes. Try using vibrato on the sustained note, and understand that if one note has intention and depth, you will project something meaningful that extends the expression of the improvised line.

Pick a buzzword such as "excited," then write down that word and an additional nine words. Give the list to a friend, and play your improvised line with the character of "excited," and then ask your friend to pick the word that best associates what he heard with what you played. The hope is that through experimentation, you will be able to project in the least amount of notes your intended character.

*Aesthetic Exercise Step 3: Practice*

If you can feel and experience emotion when you listen to music, you can express emotion and feelings and ideas to others while performing it. But you have to work on it just like you work on the technique of your instrument. Just like any other learned technique, developing aesthetics in your improvisation must be practiced.

## Step 3A: *Start with the notes*

1. Begin by improvising a line of music. It can be as short as an eight-bar phrase.
2. Record it.
3. Transcribe yourself, writing the notes you created on a piece of blank staff paper.
4. Take the written notes and discover the musical nuances of what you just composed.
5. Write within each phrase a word that says what you want to express.
6. Perform the piece again as if you are performing a work composed by someone other than you. Focus your mind on the character, not the notes. Accentuate the expression.
7. Now take all of the labels placed on each phrase, and think of the antonym of each word.
8. On a separate piece of staff paper, write only the words (the ones opposite of the original words you wrote).
9. Record yourself playing music that represents only the words.
10. Listen back and see if you were able to portray the words you wrote down.

Does it sound the way you intended it to sound? If the answer is yes, congratulations! If the answer is no, go back and start with a brand-new improvisation and do the exercise again.

## Step 3B: *Start with the words*

1. Begin by writing down a series of words.
   For example: Happy, Sad, Angry, Depressed
2. Improvise and record a melody based on the character of those words.
3. Transcribe yourself on a piece of blank staff paper, writing the notes you just improvised.

| Happy | Sad | Angry | Depressed |
|---|---|---|---|

4. Perform the piece again as if you are performing a work composed by someone other than you. Focus your mind on the character, not the notes. Accentuate the expression.
5. Now take all of the labels placed on each phrase, and think of the antonym of each word.
6. On a separate piece of staff paper, write only those words (the ones opposite of the original words you wrote).

| Sad | Happy | Pleased | Jubilant |
|---|---|---|---|

7. Improvise and record a melody based on the character of those words.

*Aesthetic Exercise Step 4: Mind Expansion*

Another effective approach to constructing creative lines is to read. There is a multitude of benefits to reading. Concerning its effects on constructing a creative musical line, reading helps stimulate the brain, gives more knowledge to a subject, and improves memory, focus, and concentration—all areas that assist in creating improvisation.

For example: If the piece you are improvising is about or connected to the American Revolution, research facts about the American Revolution.

1. Read books about the revolution.
2. Answer questions such as
   Who are the key players?
   Why did it start?
   Why did it end?
   Why did the key players do what they did?
   What feelings could the key figures have when going through the event?
   How can those feelings then be related and projected via one's instrument?
3. Always go to the source when researching, and take mental notes. Be meticulous with the researched material, and chart out the most important events.
4. Strive to have a central theme and be confident that the musical line created best represents the element.
5. Try to improvise short melodies representing each of the answers. For example:
   George Washington: theme
   George Washington at the beginning of the war: confident
   George Washington in the middle of the war: unsure
   George Washington at the end of the war: relieved

*In a Creative Slump?*

Discovering the complexity behind an improvised phrase is a collaboration between the invented notes, how the notes groove with others, and the meaning behind the notes. Sometimes this collaboration is difficult to maintain. Some musicians will inevitably fall into a rut within an improvisational form such as a fake tune. How then does one handle falling into a creative slump? I once asked Byron Stripling what the best way was to handle a creative depression. His answer: "Avoid one."

Strive to be at the highest artistic level. High-level creative people limit the amount of uninspired experiences because they are always thinking of new ways to create. They also rarely fall into a routine and do things just because they are convenient. They constantly push themselves to go further than they did in the past and always look for ways to step into the deep. However, if you experience an artistic low point, you should contemplate simple solutions to solve the complex issues involved with a creative slump. One solution is focusing on a single area of music. I have found that by doing this, my mind gives me the space needed to explore and experiment with the multiple dimensions of that chosen area.

When you find yourself in a rut, focus on, for example, harmony. Explore only the harmony and see how far outside of the harmony you can take your solo, then bring it back around to the tonic key. Or focus only on playing guide tones and see if you can create exciting melodies with only the guide tones. Also, consider the idea that good improvisers should surround themselves with great improvisers. Being around great improvisers will inspire and motivate in such a way that a weaker improviser will naturally heighten his own creative experience. By embracing the ideas of better improvisers, weaker improvisers will naturally progress to the next creative level. For example, listen to the solos of other players in the jazz band. By listening and then "stealing" their ideas, an improviser can incorporate the ideas of others, stimulating one's own creative process. Another tactic to get out of a creative slump is to draw upon material from one's own experiences. For each improvisation, the goal is to have the ideas evolve. If the same notes are used in concurrent phrases, do not play them the same exact way. Play them differently so the music can evolve and grow toward its conclusion.

### Other ways to get out of a creative slump

- Stop playing. The solo is over. If you have nothing else to say, then don't say anything else.
- Play the idea again and utilize triplets instead of eighth notes.
- Add a tritone substitution on V7 chords.
- Quote a transcribed solo from your favorite improvisational artist.
- Start lines on the upbeats—no downbeats.
- Play the idea again, but this time take it down an octave or up an octave.
- Incorporate extended techniques of your instrument.
- Challenge yourself to begin and end your lines on the third of every chord (or any other specific note).
- Sing an improvised chorus instead of playing it on your instrument.
- Use more space: Play for four bars, rest for four bars.
- Improvise only playing on the offbeat.
- Use the intervals or rhythm of a transcribed line as a motif for your solo.
- Read a book and then improvise the soundtrack to the story.
- Take a break for a few minutes, leave the practice room, and then come back to it.
- Listen to music.

### Essential Elements Applied When Creating a Compelling Solo

#### 1. Trust

I once played in a classical improvising chamber ensemble with a cellist, flute, and trombone player. The roles are blurred in this type of ensemble and certainly not set in stone. If these musicians came together without any rehearsing and decided to improvise, it would be hard at first to determine who was doing what. It is hard because the trumpet player can create the melody as easily as a flute player would. And a trombone player can create a harmonic bass line as easily as a cellist would. In this scenario, you have to trust how each instrument will complement the other, coupled with the personalities of the people playing those instruments.

#### 2. Ability to Listen

Improvisation, like a conversation, also involves active *listening*. An active listener in improvised music is always made aware of her musical surroundings and knows the direction of the piece.

A key quality that active listeners avoid is denial. When an improviser provides a gift of an idea, it is best to accept the idea and develop it. This development may turn into something completely different, but keep in mind that the one who starts a musical line is establishing something. It is inappropriate to reject the phrase, motif, or idea that another improviser brings to the musical table. This creates a problem, whether caused by nervousness or an improviser's desire to do their own idea instead of the presented idea. Conflict, in general, is good because it can drive toward resolution; however, when one improviser is going in one direction, and another improviser wants to go in a different direction, this can throw off the creative process and destroy the creative mood.

## 3. Synergize

Years ago, studying with Jim Carroll, I discovered that working as a team and seeing the bigger picture as a group is more important than individual success. Players who *synergize* their efforts will create a piece of music that is stronger than anything they could have come up with on their own. A genuinely exceptional improviser is someone who seamlessly executes the understanding of how to lead and follow at the same time.

## 4. Micro- and Macromanagement

Something to consider when practicing improvisational musical phrases is having both a *micro and macro* viewpoint. A portion of the improviser's brain needs to be thinking about the overall harmonic progression and how the lines created relate. They should also be thinking about the overall artistic effect of what they are trying to convey. Tangentially, improvisers must have a micro view and project how smaller phrases connect to one another to create an entire solo. They need to think about the articulation, style, dynamics, and swing of the phrase. When constructing a phrase, combining both a micro and macro view will instill a compositional perspective in your solo. This outlook will impart a mental awareness where the improviser invents a solo with more of a composer's viewpoint (broader perspective) instead of just trying to sound good for herself (narrow-minded, self-centered solo).

## 5. Realization

Mr. Carter told me years ago that in order to construct a musical line, an improviser "must be in a state of musical meditation where the creator's technique is aligned with his imagination." When creating improvisational musical lines with other people, each player's role is similar to a role played in a meaningful conversation. A quality conversation involves asking good questions and not making it about oneself. In music, this is similar to a rhythm section creating a groove that allows the soloist the opportunity to respond accordingly or a bassoon player playing a bass line that demands another musician respond by playing a melody on top.

## 6. Stepping into the Deep

When comparing chamber music improvisation to a conversation, going further and *stepping into the deep* end of the conversation will heighten the level of musical interest. A great conversation goes beyond the surface of "Hello, how are you?" Instead, it asks, "Hello, tell me about the worst part of your day." The latter asks more profound questions, resulting in deeper answers and a deeper connection. Musically, this means an improviser should create a line that contains musical integrity. An ensemble should be on the same proverbial page when communicating the intent of the piece. Then each individual musician invents lines that help contribute to the intent. Thinking about improvising at this level will help musicians transcend the boundaries of chords and scales or what to play and what not to play. It will focus on the value of what needs to be said using the chords and scales as the vocabulary.

## 7. Confidence

Part of inventing a compelling solo is to have confidence that what you are saying makes a point musically. The point needs to be clear, concise, and contribute to the overall conversation with the other improvising musicians.

## 8. Genuine Study of Craft

Since the improvisational form is freer than pre-composed music, it may be hard for novice improvisers to understand how to separate themselves from their instrument's role. In time and with a lot of practice and self-reflection, an improviser will be able to separate himself from the instrument and do the job needed in the moment. For example, I can remember a time in an improvised concert where the cellist in the group began performing a melody, and immediately the trombone player began performing a countermelody. I was confident, in that moment, that the piece needed a bass line. Now as a trumpet player who rarely plays the bass line, it was hard to have the confidence to play a bass line like a bass player adequately. However, through years of study, I had a deep understanding of the capabilities and limitations of my instrument. So, instead of sounding like a bass player, I allowed the other players in the group to feed me creative ideas that I could support in such a way that acted as a bass line.

## 9. Practice

In Kenny Werner's book *Effortless Mastery*, he quotes Bobby McFerrin, saying, "Improvisation is the courage to move from one note to the next." Werner goes on to say, "Once you conquer that basic fear, when you are able to make that leap from one note to the next without thinking or preparing for it, then you are improvising." A compelling solo comes from years of practicing thinking and preparing, followed by years of performing without thinking and preparing. An improviser needs to put the time in to condition the muscle memory so that the relationship between intention to invention becomes second nature. As a result, when an improviser performs, the instrument becomes an extension of the mind.

## 10. Imagination

If developing improvisers think they need more exercises in imagination, then I would recommend Bruce Adolphe's book *The Mind's Ear*. According to Mr. Adolphe, "The exercises in this book cover a wide range of techniques and approaches to engaging the musical imagination, including suggestions for imagining music in silence that one may do alone, performance games for the solo player, group games with and without instruments, games involving a wide variety of improvisation procedures, and experiments in musical imagining that involve composing."

The more improvisers inevitably attempt to make a solo more compelling, the more they will be forced to look into more stylistically appropriate choices based on the performed genre. Once there is a connection between the importance of developing the how to and what to improvise, the final step is for the musician to discover how to apply this connection to a particular genre. How can a musician unlock the secret to applying the concepts learned to a particular genre? What follows are applications of intention and invention to multiple genres. The next chapters will explore the third and final step of my three-step process to learn improvisation—a process I have called *application*.

# 8 Understanding Jazz Language

An Introduction to Decoding the Symbols for Jazz Improvisation

Students I have taught in the past who come from a "play by ear" background may resist studying theory and harmony. They have suggested to me that if they begin to give a name to concepts they naturally employ, their analysis will obstruct their freedom and spontaneity. To a certain extent, these students are correct. I believe that those who listen and mimic the sound as opposed to first learning what scale works with a particular chord have an advantage. However, we live in a world that anchors itself on the visual, requiring, at times, to create music using chord symbols. Therefore, understanding jazz's language involves studying theoretical concepts so that improvisers can adequately comprehend the harmonic guidelines to communicate their ideas.

Chord symbol comprehension is similar to understanding road signs when driving. Road signs regulate the flow of traffic and direct drivers where they want to go. Chord symbols guide improvisers through the harmonic maze in a similar fashion. However, road signs are not the critical factor in getting the driver to his arrival point—his car, understanding how to drive, ability to follow directions, and intuition get him to where he wants to go. The signs are only there to guide the driver along the way. Chord symbols serve the same function: They provide the necessary information for the improviser to express his solo or denote how to voice his chords. Improvisers use their instrument and their understanding of improvisation to play a solo, but the symbols bracket the piece's harmony and provide a clear road map to great improvisation. This chapter discusses how to comprehend chord symbols and how to use them to help spontaneously create improvisation.

Some classical musicians see jazz chord symbols and become overwhelmed with the visual; it interrupts their natural ability to improvise. Also, for some jazz musicians, seeing the symbols may cause them to focus too much on scales or licks or possibly what notes correlate with the provided chord, and they ultimately miss the point of spontaneous jazz improvisation. Think of improvisation as an act that communicates an idea. The symbols are only there to help an improviser spontaneously create music within the framework of the progression.

It is important to not focus too much on the "words" of the conversation (the notes) but to arrive at a place of awareness that situates the mind to focus on expression, only using the "words" as a tool to help express the point. Imagine one person talking to another person. Once a person develops a specific vocabulary and grammar level, she no longer thinks about how words construct to create sentences. She only focuses on the point she is trying to make and uses her vocabulary as a tool for expression. The improviser's role is to take the information given and communicate it so that the expressed idea shines through. Now we need to ask, When one is reading a book, or in this case, chord progressions, how does one comprehend the symbols quickly enough to spontaneously express a point of view, idea, or thought in real time?

## Improvisation for the Jazz Soloist: The Signs and Symbols of the Language of Jazz Improvisation

### *What Is the Point of Chord Symbols?*

The point is to express to improvisers the harmony that will occur over any given measure. The improviser's role is to bring purpose and life experiences alongside the chord symbols. The intersection of the improviser's invention and the chord symbol's information gives a proper grasp of the overall chord progression and its tangential purposes. The symbols are just ciphers to translate. This is why multiple players can play different solos over the same chord changes in the same song. Each musician comes to the table with different ideas to express and different points of view and sound concepts that translate the symbols into a reality that others can understand.

### *So How Does One Become Better at Understanding Chord Symbols?*

First, build a solid technical foundation on the chosen instrument to have the means to express the desired sound. Second, learn and then be able to implement at will a large jazz vocabulary. Third, set a purpose for the solo, and identify the expression. Fourth, engage in aural exercises that will aid in quickly being able to identify the sound of chords. Fifth, be a time traveler, executing in the present yet building on previous material to create new and robust meaning while setting up what is to come in the future. Sixth, engage in self-awareness—record yourself playing and seek out methods to improve comprehension.

### *How to Learn Chord Symbol Comprehension*

Know that it is not about learning what scale to play over the chord; instead, it is about hearing what the chord sounds like in relationship to the other chords. This relationship helps the player use the chord progression as a foundation to play notes representing the emotion.

Aurally identify the three most common chord symbols—the major seventh, minor seventh, and dominant seventh chord.

### *The Major Seventh Chord*

The first step to dissecting the meaning of jazz chord symbols begins with the major seventh chord. This symbol essentially means that the most important notes within this sound are the first, third, fifth, and seventh scale degrees. Playing these notes simultaneously creates a specific sound that the improviser must recognize as the major seven sound. Once the improviser can recognize this sound, or better yet, anticipate what it will sound like, she can begin to improvise. Begin by creating short, simple melodies utilizing the tools discussed in previous chapters. The best way to decode the major seventh chord is by recognizing the symbol and associating that symbol with the major seventh sound.

Notice in the previous example how the chord tones are primarily on the downbeat. Nonchord tones, notes a half step away, and accidentals are all on the upbeat. When dealing with the major seventh chord, avoid using the blues scale, the sharp nine, and the dominant seven scale (mixolydian). These three things do not work over the major seventh chord—they work well with the Bb dominant seven chord. Using chromaticism on the upbeats to get to the chord tone on the downbeat is very good. Break up the solo into four-bar phrases. Not sure of a phrase's definition? To understand the meaning of a phrase, think of it as if writing a sentence. The phrase should have a clear beginning and ending point with a sense of purpose. Remember, jazz improvisation is composing in real time. Take the time to slowly write things out to help ingrain these concepts to prepare for the opportunity to compose or (improvise) in real time.

The improviser must understand that what one plays on the downbeat is fundamental to good improvisation. An analysis of Charlie Parker's improvisation will lead the learner to notice that Parker plays mostly anything on the upbeat but plays a chord tone on the downbeat. Try this in your solo, and see if it makes sense to your ear.

The following are good choices to make when dealing with the major seven:

- Avoid the tonic.
- Start your phrases with the third or fifth.
- Play chord tones on the downbeat.
- Play nonchord tones, chromatic notes, and accidentals on the upbeat.
- Avoid using the blues scale, the sharp nine, and the dominant seven.
- Break up your solo into four-bar phrases.
- Keep things simple and singable.

If there is a problem with trying to figure out where to start or what "words to use in your musical sentence," here is a suggestion. These are a couple of "words," or what the jazz guys like to call "licks," to use to help get you started. This lick sounds good because it starts on the seventh, outlines the major chord, and ends on the third. This can be your all-purpose jazz lick.

## *The Minor Seventh Chord*

After significant practice resulting in a high level of confident improvisation over the major seventh sound, it is time to discover the minor seventh sound. The minor seventh sound involves a chord that emphasizes a natural minor scale's first, third, fifth, and seventh scale degree. Most of the time, whenever one sees a minor seventh chord, it will typically function as a ii chord. This chord is a ii chord because it builds off the second scale degree of the major scale. If the minor seventh chord functions as a ii chord, it is wise to utilize a sound that best matches the sonority—the Dorian scale. For example, if an improviser sees a D minor chord, he or she should play the D Dorian scale. The most significant difference between the major I chord and the minor ii chord other than tonality is the use of notes. In a major I chord, the improviser should avoid certain notes, such as the fourth. Improvisers do not need to worry about dissonance or avoid certain diatonic notes in a minor ii chord since all minor scale tones are consonant. The best way to decode the minor seventh chord is to recognize the symbol and associate that symbol with the minor seventh sound.

### *The Dominant Seventh Chord*

The next and final chord to begin understanding the language of jazz is the dominant chord. Theorists call it the dominant chord because the relationship between intervals built on the dominant scale degree of a given key (e.g., G7 in the key of C major) tends to pull towards the root (C). The dominant seventh chord is useful to improvisers because it has a major triad with a powerful sound that also includes a tritone between the third and seventh of the chord (e.g., the interval between B—the third of the chord and F—the seventh of the chord is a tritone). In a diatonic context, the third of the chord is the leading tone of the scale (B—third of the chord is the seventh scale degree of the C major scale), which, as earlier stated, tends to pull towards the root (C). This pull creates a satisfying resolution with which to end a piece.

### *The ii-V-I Progression*

The most important progression of sound in jazz is the ii-V-I chord progression. In a major key, the ii-V-I progression consists of three chords beginning with a minor seventh chord followed by a dominant seventh chord and ending with a major chord. If you practiced each chord individually, it would make playing over the combination of all three easier.

The subsequent diagram represents a ii-V-I in the key of C:

| ii: Dmin7 | V: G7 | I: Cmajor7 |
|---|---|---|
| *scale:* D Dorian | *scale:* G mixolydian | *scale:* C major |

The scales typically learned for these chords are Dorian for the minor two, mixolydian for the dominant, and major for the major. However, the improviser needs to think about these scales not as a scale played when a particular chord happens but rather internalize the sound of a ii-V and play the sound. Or if playing three scales sounds overwhelming, instead think about this: These scales are modes of the C major scale, so when you see a ii-V progression in a major key, you can play the major scale of the I chord for the whole progression—just start on a different scale degree. A major scale makes it a bit easier to construct lines that lead from one chord to the next. As the improviser becomes more confident with this progression, she can emphasize certain parts of the major scale when a particular chord is requested. For example,

*Pentatonic, Blues, and the Seven/Three Resolution*

Improvisers must have in their arsenal a variety of tools to respond to the chord symbol information—items such as the pentatonic scale, blues scale, modes, and grasping the seven/three resolution.

*The Pentatonic Scale*

The pentatonic scale is a collection of five notes derived from the Greek word *pente*, meaning five and *tonic*, meaning tone. If the chord is a D minor seventh, then the pentatonic scale played would be D F G A C.

Once you master the minor pentatonic scale, try looking at the major pentatonic. A great way to comprehending a chord is using a pentatonic scale in a pattern or sequence of melodic or rhythmic ideas.

## The Blues Scale

Going a step further from the minor pentatonic scale, add one more note. The result will be the creation of the blues scale. For example, add an Ab to the D minor pentatonic scale, thus creating this scale: D F G Ab A C.

Jazz improvisers typically refer to the added note as a crunch note—also known as the blue note. When first learning how to use the blues scale, try not to stay on the crunch note for an extended period of time. Think of this crunch note like a chromatic passing tone used for dissonance and resolution techniques, just like one would ornament a Baroque phrase. The blues scale is a form of the pentatonic scale—practice playing in sequences and patterns to color the chord.

## Using the Blues Scale

A great way to learn to use the blues scale is to break it in half. If a tune is in the key of F, it means you play the F blues scale. It is important to note that you play this scale over the entire form of the blues. Do not change scales when the chord changes.

For example: Don't play the Bb blues scale when the chord changes to Bb.

Instead, continue to play the F blues scale even when it changes to Bb.

What changes is the part of the scale to emphasize. The emphasized part depends on the chord. Certain notes are better at accentuating the chord change without changing the scale.

The circled notes above are a better choice when playing over the F7 chord. Notice the notes emphasized: The root, fifth, and seventh.

These circled notes above, however, are a better choice when playing over the Bb7 chord. Notice here what notes to emphasize: The root, fifth, and seventh of the Bb chord.

Strive not to change the tonality. The tonality of the blues is F, and by changing scales when the chord changes, we have changed the tonality of the piece. So, if the F blues scale plays over the entire piece, the same sense of the bluesy tonality is kept while the chord changes underneath. The key center stays the same; therefore, when the chords changes, the improviser needs to make the scale work with the new chord. Making the scale work with the new chord keeps the tonality.

The downfall of beginning improvisers is thinking, *Play the blues scale, and it will work over the twelve bars.* If they do, they will inevitably play up and down the scale without regard to the chord changes that occur.

**Example of a flawed young blues solo:**

Remember: Just because the chords change doesn't necessarily mean the tonality does. The previous example is typical of what young improvisers all do. They start on the root, play the lowered third, fourth, and add the blue note. And by the time we get to the IV chord, students play the root of that chord and so on.

**Example of a better use of the blues scale:**

This example is a good blues solo. Notice its use of the blues scale. In the first measure (I), the improviser uses the upper part of the blues scale. In the second measure (IV), the improviser uses the lower part of the blues scale. Notice the use of two-bar phrases. I outline the chords starting on the seventh in a sequential pattern in the ninth and tenth measures. Pay particular attention to the last measure. Nothing is happening in this measure. Nothing can be a good thing. Utilizing space in your solo is a good habit to develop. Encourage your students not to feel the need to play all the time.

88  *Understanding Jazz Language*

*Blues and the Seven/Three Resolution*

The blues is a form of music that contains a repetitive pattern in a twelve-bar structure. The twelve-bar blues is typically a set of three different chords played over a twelve-bar scheme:

I    I    I    I    IV    IV    I    I    V    IV    I    V or I

In analyzing this blues solo, we must start with the fourth measure. Look at the fourth measure and ask yourself what the improviser is doing. The improviser plays a C in this bar. He avoids playing a C until this point because, in the next measure, he plays a B, which is a seven-three resolution. This is a textbook way to avoid playing the resolution until the fifth measure.

On the fourth bar of a blues progression, the dominant chord has a dominant function. The first three chords function as a bluesy tonic, and in the fourth measure, it functions as dominant. There are various ways that seven chords function. They can function as a one ($I^7$) or a two ($ii^7$) or, in this case, a dominant ($V^7$).

You can tell that it functions as a dominant because your ear tells you it wants to resolve. A dominant chord that has a dominant function will always resolve. There is no resolution in the first three measures. If you try to use the first three measures as a dominant chord, you'll be setting up for a resolution that is not happening yet. So the resolution only occurs from the fourth measure into the fifth measure. The first measure could technically function as a dominant resolving to the second bar F7, but typically jazz players play bluesy stuff in the first three measures, and then in the fourth measure, it will function as a dominant chord leading to the fifth measure. Take a look at the ninth measure:

Notice the classic technique of encircling the most important note. The improviser encircles the third of the chord, the most important note. He creates tension and then resolves the chord. Look at the tenth measure:

He does the same thing to the C#. He encircles the most important note, causing tension and resolution. He could have eliminated this and just played the C#, and it still would have sounded good, but he delays the resolution until the downbeat of the third beat. Think that's all that's going

on here? ... Wait, there's more! He puts in a flat nine, the Bb; it's not a minor second, it's a flat nine. It's not augmented, it's not mixolydian, it's another scale that introduces the flat nine that you can use on the dominant chord. It's a diminished scale starting on the half step—G Ab Bb B C# D E F. Classical musicians call this scale octatonic.

If a chord functions as a dominant, you can play a mixolydian scale (also known as a dominant scale), an augmented triad, or an octatonic scale. You can tell a chord functions as a dominant because the next chord is a one. In blues, the fourth measure functions as a dominant because the next chord could be the I of a new tonal center. The next time we see a dominant chord is in the tenth measure.

*Seven/Three Resolution—Reprise!*

The third and seventh of every chord distinguish and individualize the sound of the chord. Emphasizing these notes in your improvisation will help guide your compositions to accurately imply how the chord changes. A great way to practice knowing how to resolve the seven and the three is looking at this:

The first measure functions as a ii, so a Dorian sound is made, outlining chord tones on the downbeat. The seven in this measure occurs on beat four, resolving to a C# (third) of A7 in the next bar. This new chord functions as a V. We now play right down the scale alluding to a resolution to I. By the last measure, we end the phrase on the ninth instead of the root. Not playing the root isn't wrong; it is just that the ninth is a better choice to make. It sounds more like jazz and less like Haydn.

*The Secret Hidden Harmonic Code*

There is a hidden harmonic melody that is in every song. Most jazz compositions ever written since the 20th century have their own hidden harmonic melody to it. And if you can find that harmonic melody and play it, you will be able to play an excellent improvised solo. This hidden melody tells you what the important notes are, and this section will tell you how to find that hidden melody. The harmonic melody is a series of notes that guide your ear from chord to chord. The notes are typically the third and the seventh scale degree of the chord. These notes should be included in your solo. They are also great notes to help you connect one bar to the next. The use and understanding of guide tones are an important part of learning to improvise clearly on the kind of harmonic framework used by jazz musicians.

Here is the secret hidden harmonic melody for the blues:

That's the universal hidden melody for the blues. Every song with multiple chord changes has a hidden melody. Incorporating these notes into your solo is important to make it sound like you are playing the changes. How chords are related is this idea of tension and resolution. The guide tones are the third and the seventh of the chord. So if we start with a seven, this creates tension, and we resolve that tension by playing the third of the next chord. The guide tones break the blues down to its lowest common denominator.

The best way to incorporate this secret melody into your solo is as follows:

Base your solo around this harmonic melody in the first three measures of your solo. In the fourth measure, the chord functions as a dominant, so you can play a multitude of note choices there (in this case, the lowered seventh). In the fifth and sixth bars, you can play bluesy tonic stuff. In the seventh and eighth measures, play the guide tone lines. Then in the ninth, tenth, and eleventh measures are your ii-V-I. The final measure is the five chord leading back to the top of the progression so that you can play notes (outlining A, C#, E, G) that help drive back to the tonic, or in this case, nothing at all.

Take a look at this written solo:

The first measure outlines the secret harmonic melody starting on the third (F# in D7). The third resolves by basing the solo on the seventh in the second measure chord (F in G7). The solo is back to being based on the third in the next measure (F# in D7). In the fourth measure, the improviser only plays one note. It is the seventh, which is the most important note in that measure. Bluesy stuff is played in the next two measures, followed by the seventh and eighth measures going back to outlining the guide tone lines (F# and C natural). Then in the ninth, tenth, and eleventh, a ii-V-I line is played.

## *Putting it All Together*

There is a distinct sound between a classical player and a jazz player. The choices in the way they shape notes and the way they play a phrase is entirely different. If the same phrase is given to both types of players, they will play the phrase in different ways. How can a classical player learn how to play a phrase like a jazz player? Answer: Listen and then record yourself. If you are trying to copy the style of someone else, record yourself. Transcribe what they are playing, and then record yourself playing it. After this, stop and listen to the recording you just made of yourself and ask yourself if it sounds the same as the jazz artist you are trying to mimic. If it doesn't, then keep going until it does. Ask the question: Do I sound the way I want to? This method of practice will speed up the transformation of a classical player playing in a jazz style.

To dissect how the jazz player would play swing is extremely difficult to verbalize. To combat this dilemma, listen to a variety of jazz sounds. This process will give you more tools to help you develop your own sound. A big challenge that most educators have a problem with is teaching the concept of swing. It is difficult to explain how to swing eighth notes. Well, here's the thing: *You can't explain how to swing!*

At the start, some beginners may experience a very structured, technical analysis of how to swing, like making sure the student doesn't do the dotted eighth sixteenth or making sure the student accents the upbeat instead of the downbeat. There is also explaining the concept of using the triplet pattern, tying the first two triplet notes together, and playing your eighths that way. This concept is bad because it is too close to the dotted eighth sixteenth. As John Thomas told me, "Forget all of these concepts; it is all just a quick fix on how to swing. Instead, listen more. Listen to the nuance of how a professional swings."

As a final thought, compare learning the jazz style to learning to speak. Young infants do not have the ability to read or write; instead, they listen to their parents talk and absorb that information. It is the same in jazz; it is difficult to explain how to swing in a technical way. The best way to learn to swing is to listen to recordings and mimic exactly how they play. Trust in the ability to listen to something and learn it by ear. *After all, you can speak, right? You learned that by ear!*

### *The Bebop Scale*

The bebop scale is frequently used in jazz improvisation and derived from the modes of the major scale. There are three types of frequently used bebop scales: the bebop dominant scale, the bebop Dorian scale, and the bebop major scale.

Bebop Dominant Scale

Bebop Dorian Scale

Bebop Major Scale

Each of these scales has an extra chromatic passing tone. When the dominant chord functions as a V7 in any song, we can play the dominant scale, bebop scale, or play the major third over that chord, and it will sound great. One could also incorporate the tritone sub or play the melodic minor scale up a half step.

92    *Understanding Jazz Language*

### *The Blues Scale Recap*

The blues scale, as previously discussed, is a version of the pentatonic scale. As classical musicians know, Debussy and Ravel used the pentatonic and whole-tone scales as a mechanism for nonresolution. The blues scale works the same way. There is no resolution when only using the blues scale. So when you get to the V7 chord, veer away from the blues scale and play something that outlines the V7 chord, especially utilizing the third or seventh scale degree. Think of playing the blues in this way: How can I implement a certain sound (the blues scale) over a particular set of chord changes? How does "the F blues sound" fit over the blues chord progression? Specific notes are better suited for certain chords within the progression. For example, don't start with F when playing the blues scale. The F is not a wrong note; it is just that there are better choices. Technically, the F will work, but it gives too much information and is not that interesting to the jazz ear. But if you start with the notes C, Eb, and F and go up the scale from that point, then you have the five, the seven, and the one, which makes for a much more interesting solo. By playing it this way, we outline the important notes, the five and the seven. We would also highlight the third, but there is no third in the blues scale, and our job is to create the blues sound over the chord changes. Thus, the root, the seven, and the five are better notes to start with at the beginning of your blues solo. Whenever you study jazz, don't think of notes as wrong or right. Think of notes as one choice being better than another choice.

### *Essential Elements Applied When Learning the Jazz Language*

### 1. Trust

Trust that after a certain period of time spent conditioning the mind to understand the symbols quickly, improvisers will develop second nature. Second nature is a place in improviser's development that involves instantly hearing a note in relation to the visual chord without much thought. Trust that the process to decode the language of jazz will take the same amount of time it takes to decode any other learned foreign language.

### 2. Ability to Listen

A well-known story begins in Stuttgart, Germany, where a young Herbie Hancock and famed jazz musician Miles Davis were playing together. One night during a performance of "So What," Herbie played a chord that did not belong in the chord progression. Miles paused for a moment and then began to play notes in his solo that made Herbie's chord mistake sound correct. Most people would hear this as Miles's ability to create something right out of something wrong, but Miles did not hear this chord as a mistake. Miles heard it as something that happened—an event, a part of the reality happening at that moment. Since he did not see it as a mistake, he felt that it was his responsibility to create something that fit. Miles had a mind that was open enough to accept what was happening in the moment; he accepted things for what they were and then responded by turning them into something constructive. This deep understanding of jazz language derives from an open mind and actively listening to one's environment.

## 3. Synergy

The collaboration between musicians in the jazz idiom is vital to the successful performance of this type of music. Improvisers are always synergizing their roles to create something bigger than themselves.

## 4. Micromanagement and Macromanagement

When it comes to chord recognition, I focus my attention on both the micro and macro levels. This ideal recognition is via the ear. At the micro level, an improviser must be able to aurally recognize the individual chords and respond by utilizing the notes that make the most musical sense. They must also recognize how chords connect to one another on the macro level, creating a chord progression that harmonizes a melody not yet created.

## 5. Realization

To understand the jazz language, improvisers must realize and let go of what they see, rely on what they hear, and respond accordingly. The response must match elements such as style, rhythm, time, articulation, proper chord voicings, etc.

## 6. Stepping into the Deep

At this point, I would encourage you to seek out more advanced levels of jazz improvisation. Step into the deep of how John Coltrane extends harmony, or how Ornette Coleman explores the free form, dense textures of avant-garde/free jazz, or perhaps the difference between early Chicago style collective improvisation versus early New Orleans collective improvisation.

## 7. Confidence

When first learning to decode the language of jazz, it is perfectly natural to feel apprehensive. Most beginning improvisers become overwhelmed when introduced to chord symbols and then expected to play notes that do not exist on the sheet music. As you work on decoding the language, have confidence in what you do know but also what you don't know. For many students, I've discovered that over the course of playing an improvised jazz solo, if there is 75% that they do not understand, they allow the 25% they do know to fall prey to insecurities.

## 8. Genuine Study of Craft

Improvisers must study the various symbols associated with jazz improv. It is not enough to recognize the symbols and know what notes would be acceptable to play; rather, improvisers should be able to see the chord symbols visually, hear what the chord sounds like, and then mentally conceive a melody, rhythm, or harmony.

## 9. Practice

There is a big difference between knowing what to play and hearing what to play. For example, when you look at a C7 chord, you may understand visually that an improviser could play most notes that fall within a C major scale with a lowered seventh. However, if you can't hear what the chord sounds like and cannot respond accordingly, you are not utilizing your practice time in the most efficient way. Practicing what to play is important, just like practicing one's vocabulary in an English class. However, if you only practice vocabulary and not put the vocabulary in context, you will do yourself a disservice. You need to make sure you prioritize practicing the ability to hear the sound of each chord in the progression.

## 10. Imagination

The most important concept to glean is to imagine the sound of the visual symbols on the lead sheet. Strive to develop a vivid imagination of what notes could sound appropriate over the sound of the chord.

# 9 Crossing Over

## Jazz Improvisation for the Classical Musician

In the world of jazz music, Louis Armstrong had already transcended the referential solo by 1925, Thelonious Monk showed how to unfold motific development over multiple choruses, and John Coltrane could make any phrase into a virtuosic etude. Studying the work of these masters takes a tremendous amount of study and practice. Some may suggest that the entry point of creating an improvised solo cannot be found in a book, rather it is what's on the masters' recordings. To a certain extent, this statement is true! Listening and imitation is a fantastic way to help a young musician learn to mimic their favorite professional musician. However, a beginner listening to and internalizing John Coltrane's solo to *Giant Steps*, for example, may be overwhelming. Is there a way to help those just starting out and prepare them to eventually memorize and internalize the masters?

Regardless of genre, the most intriguing solos are those in which performers are able to musically articulate what is first mentally heard or conceived, allowing the physical manifestation of the musical idea to occur. In lessons, classical musicians learn the concept of mentally envisioning the sound before playing it. Classical musicians visualize the sound in situations such as rehearsing in the practice room, performing a solo in a recital, performing with an ensemble, etc. Jazz musicians also must conceptualize the sound they desire to create, effectively performing the same mental process as classical musicians—the only difference being a lack of written music and sound concept. For example, jazz musicians begin their improvisation by mentally hearing and developing a melody that adequately conveys their feelings, creates the desired sound, and connects to the tune's harmonic progression in real time. They understand the chord progression and use their learned vocabulary to take part in the musical conversation. Just like any newly introduced concept, mentally conceiving a melody and then articulating it in a jazz dialect is a skill that needs time to develop. This chapter aims to assist in building the necessary auditory foundation to successfully convert an improvisation created by a classical musician into a solo constructed in the language of jazz. So, how does one hope to do this successfully?

### Step 1: Beginning to Cross Over

#### *Exercise #1: Conceptualize*

The first step is to begin with something known by all musicians: The concert Bb scale. Improvise a simple melody using the notes of the concert Bb scale. At this point, the improviser should not be concerned with what note to play over which chord, the correct style, etc.—just play.

DOI:10.4324/9781003341857-9

Step 1: Set metronome at quarter note equals 60.
Step 2: Play a concert Bb major 7 chord.
Step 3: Hear a melody that fits in the concert Bb major 7 chord over the course of two bars.
Step 4: Listen for every aspect of that melody: Can you hear the exact rhythm?, can you hear the exact notes?, can you hear the articulation, etc.
Step 5: Transcribe what you hear in your head and play it on your instrument.
Step 6: Ask yourself, did what you play match what you heard in your head? If yes, move on to the next step; if not, go back to the beginning.
Step 7: Repeat steps 1–5, but create a different melody over the course of another two bars.
Step 8: Connect the first two-bar phrase you improvised with the second two-bar phrase.
Step 9: Repeat as needed until you have reached a minimum of an eight-bar phrase in 4/4 time.
Step 10: Play the entire improvised solo.

The ultimate goal for the musician is to play with a sense of freedom and abandonment, where one can musically articulate what one conceptualizes. You will need to adjust the way you hear a melody. In making this change, the classical musician might initially feel uncomfortable; but in order to accomplish a different musical genre, one must be willing to look at different ways to conceptualize the melody within that desired dialect. Often, when given the freedom to "just play," classical musicians will instinctively play a multitude of notes when first attempting to play a jazz solo. One way to adjust is to simplify the musical phrase and reduce the number of notes.

*Exercise #2: Simplify*

Imagine that the following musical phrase is an example of what an inexperienced improviser might create using Exercise #1:

This has several positive attributes to it. However, it illustrates how an inexperienced improviser commonly tries to fill all the space with sound, including many notes without much melodic intent. A pivotal goal when introducing jazz improvisation is to play a melody an accompanying musician can understand and perhaps sing back. Remember, musicians do not simply play for themselves; rather, they play to communicate with others. Jazz is a language in and of itself that relies heavily on each member's contribution to the musical conversation. If the developing jazz improviser plays a solo that does not translate to an accompanying jazz musician, the conclusion should be that the improvised melody is too complicated and needs to be simplified. The developing improviser should try again by simplifying the melody, playing each note with purpose and direction.

Here is an example of a simplified solo:

Notice the simplicity of this melody. In contrast with the initial melody, this does not house complex rhythms or a swarm of notes. Instead, the composition of the melody follows a pleasing wavelike contour, conjunct movement, and small range with good voice leading. At this point, it is perfectly acceptable for the beginner to keep things simple and singable without playing a multitude of notes. For example:

**Please note:** Just because this is simple and singable does not make it a jazz solo. It is important to think of simple melodies. And if you think you're playing simple melodies and still feel what you're thinking isn't coming through your instrument, then simplify your thoughts more until you can match exactly what you hear in your head.

### *Exercise #3: Start with a Chord Tone*

Beginning improvisers—especially ones with a nonjazz background—may tend to hyperfocus on the tonic. In the simplified solo example, out of 21 notes, a third of them are the tonic, construed as too much emphasis on the tonic. The point here is not that the improviser did something incorrectly—rather, there may be better choices to change how an improviser hears a jazz melody.

In Bb major, a beginner's first instinct is to play Bb, as it is the note the ear is drawn to the most, making it logical that the tonic should be the acceptable and obvious note to play. In jazz, however, this is not necessarily sequitur. A seasoned jazz improviser would tend to avoid the tonic. Note: The suggestion is not that improvisers should never use the tonic, just that it be used sparingly and not emphasized at this point in development.

Imagine a chord tone depicted as the bases on a baseball field, with the tonic as home base. The tonic serves as a good starting point, but the point of being at bat is to get on base and then eventually get back home to score. For example, try improvising again, with the understanding that home base is the tonic, with first base as the third, second base as the fifth, and third base as the seventh chord tone. The developing improviser could experiment by starting phrases at a different "base" and moving to the next base/cadential point, ensuring that the completed solo ends on the home plate/tonic. Switch it up and begin playing phrases on a different base each time.

### *Exercise #4: Avoid the Tonic as a Cadential Point*

In lessons I've taught, a common problem I've noticed is that young improvisers with classically trained ears tend to target the tonic as cadential points. What should happen is that they should attempt to avoid the final resolution until the very end. By playing the tonic at a cadential point, John Thomas said to me, "The musician is telling the listener that the story is over. Think of the tonic as the 'And They Lived Happily Ever After. The End'; reserve the final resolution until the end of the improvised solo." Instead, end phrases on the third, fifth, or seventh, and end the solo on the tonic. Cadences serve the same purpose in jazz as they do in classical music. Cadences are a point in which the musical phrase is ending, but not the entire piece.

Notice how the start of each two-bar phrase begins with a chord tone, and then each phrase leads to a cadential point that does not utilize the tonic. Using nontonic cadential points along with phrases starting on a chord tone will transform your solo. Now, instead of merely playing a series of notes that may or may not work within its harmonic surroundings (in this case, Bb major), the solo begins to represent an idea that effectively communicates a melody that drives toward an end.

### *Exercise #5: Play Wrong Notes on Purpose and then Resolve them*

When hanging out with other classical musicians who are attempting jazz, some may say something along the lines of: "It's jazz, man, there are no bad notes, you play whatever you want." Someone with a limited background in jazz might believe that, but unfortunately, the root of the statement is false. The statement implies that one can play any note, and it will sound decent to the jazz ear. This is not true. There *are* bad notes in jazz—1) when the note does not belong in the chord and 2) when misused. Bad notes frequently occur even for seasoned players; however, it is how they resolve the tension the bad note creates that matters.

Beginning jazz improvisers consistently play bad notes; this is common when first attempting jazz improvisation and should not be a deterrent. In fact, the beginning improviser should feel comfortable playing the bad notes on purpose! Eventually, the ear will mature enough to identify what is pleasing and unpleasing to the jazz musician. Listening to jazz music will aid in the speed and depth of this maturity.

When purposefully playing bad notes, imagine the bad notes as being deathly poisonous cobras in a jungle. The jungle is the tonality of the solo, and the poisonous snakes are the bad notes slithering through the tonality. The poisonous snake (bad note) creates tension as it slithers close and slides through the jungle (tonality), but releases that tension as it passes by (is resolved). The point is that the snake only interrupts a small part of the jungle and does not fundamentally change the entire jungle.

Consider: How does one note sound versus another? More importantly, how does the note sound if it is resolved? The "bad" notes are simply tension. Jazz musicians capitalize on creating tension with bad notes. There is nothing wrong with playing the bad notes—they just need to be utilized wisely, as they are potentially the best notes to play *if and only if* properly resolved.

Try to lean on the bad notes. Playing a bad note will result in a development of tension, so much so that when eventually playing a chord tone, it will make the chord tone sound better than before as the resolution becomes stronger. The insinuation that there are no bad notes in jazz is false. There are bad notes. It is how we resolve the bad note that reveals either good or poor judgment. A better way of this saying should be, "It's jazz, man, there *are* bad notes. Use them to create tension or not at all!"

Here is an example:

This example sounds like the improviser does not know what she is doing. Beginning improvisers tend to be fearful, like a deer in the headlights. There is an uncertainty of what notes to play and when to play them. It can be a very humbling, embarrassing feeling to have great musical ideas expressed in one's head without the ability to produce them out of the instrument. I distinctly remember as a young classical trumpet player saying to myself, "If I just keep playing, a miracle will happen, and I'll be able to sound like Clifford Brown." The reality is, this will never happen without some guidelines.

So, there are bad notes in jazz. How the notes resolve is what matters. When performing a bad note, there is a high likelihood that a good note is a half step away. The developing improviser should play again by intentionally finding the bad notes, creating tension, and then resolving that tension by making sure to play a good note one half step away at the end of a phrase.

Here is an example:

Now that the developing improviser understands how to create tension and resolution in their solo, it is important to look for better choices.

An excellent first step in creating tension is to play chromatically to the next note; however, jazz improvisation for the classical musician is about training one's mind to hear better choices. Instead of playing stepwise in a chromatic fashion, try to encircle the chord tone. For example, use a C# and an A to create tension and resolve the Bb.

Here is an example:

Notice in this solo, the improviser plays a half step away on each side of the right note, creating tension and waiting for the right moment to resolve it. Do not overdo it, though! Do not continue to play a bad note over and over. After you play a bad note, make sure to resolve the tension. Moving between wrong notes creates a frenzy that will make the good note sound better.

Here is an example:

Notice the use of playing chromatically and resolving to the closest chord tone. Also, notice how in the fifth measure and the first two beats of the last measure, some notes do not belong in the Bb scale but followed up by resolving to chord tones. Notice in the sixth measure how the

100   *Crossing Over*

notes encircle the Bb. Grasping this concept will make improvising more interesting. Adding tension makes fearful improvisers transform into fearless ones. Be fearless!

Young classical musicians are bombarded with a plethora of choices when trying to improvise. When placing parameters around these choices, improvising becomes more manageable. Here are some parameters for the classical musician to follow:

1. **Conceptualize and transcribe what you hear.**
2. **Simplify the melody.**
3. **Start with a chord tone.**
4. **Avoid the tonic as a cadential point.**
5. **Play bad notes on purpose and then resolve them.**
6. **Encircle a chord tone, playing notes to create tension on either side.**

**Assignment:** Improvise melodies utilizing the concert Bb scale. Play without worrying about whether it sounds perfect. Conceptualize a melody in your head, and transcribe yourself by playing exactly what you hear in your head through your instrument. Then simplify your melody. Next, try to make better choices—for example, start your melody on a chord tone other than the root. Only use the tonic as a passing tone and as the final cadence of your solo. When you get comfortable playing with the Bb scale, play wrong notes (notes that fall outside of the Bb scale) on purpose, and see if you can figure out how to resolve them, whether it be by playing a half step away toward a chord tone or by encircling.

Many factors are involved with jazz improvisation—playing an instrument, thinking about the correct chord/scale relationship, playing in time, listening to the band, and being creative rather than sounding like someone who plays licks. There are ways to help isolate and exercise each aspect of jazz improvisation in order to get confident enough to go out and perform in front of people.

After you have developed a sense of play and are able to transcribe yourself, then follow some rules to help limit your choices. Remember that improvisation is composing in real time, and composing has rules. Practicing these basic rules will help the classical musician sound like a jazz improviser.

Well, hold on . . . not necessarily.

## Step 2: Got Style?

When developing jazz style, improvisers must ask themselves: Does this sound like jazz? Does that sound like Oscar Peterson, Clifford Brown, Charlie Parker, or any other jazz artist? If it doesn't, then listen to the articulation. More than likely, the improviser is not articulating every note. As a classical player, this is very natural, but the notes need to be more legato in jazz. John Thomas told me that one of the best ways to learn proper jazz phrasing is to have someone who knows the style play it as an example to emulate. He encouraged me to listen to how the expert plays a phrase and then mimic it. If an expert is not around to act as a model, then jazz recordings are essential. When listening, notice how wind players accent the upbeat and how they slur two, then tongue two while not emphasizing the downbeat. Listen to the drummer in the recording, and focus in on the ride cymbal. Try to follow the cymbal, match the rhythmic accents, and practice scales with straight eighth notes, slurring them while accenting the upbeat. As a general rule, slur everything, and every now and again, you can accent the upbeat by articulating it.

Remember: Understanding the theory of jazz and what notes to play is only half the battle. There is an intangible style to master in order to sound like a jazz improviser. I highly recommend for the beginning jazz improviser to listen to as much jazz as they can. Listening to the great jazz artists will help the young improviser develop the innate ability to play in the correct style. Imitation is the main conduit for learning to swing certain notes while others sound like straight eighth notes within the same phrase. Improvising musicians should trust their ear's ability to pick up the nuances of the expert performer. Over the course of time and diligent practice, you will develop the intangible jazz style.

Is the sound learners use for Beethoven the sound that they will use as a jazz improviser? No. So, how then is that jazz sound developed? The classical musician will need to internalize a tremendous amount of music that they might never have listened to and maybe don't actually even like very much. They will need to confront the intricacies of African rhythms that one can't even begin to notate in Western notation. So, if a classical musician is struggling with portraying the right style, I would ask them, "How much music are you listening to and imitating?"

## Step 3: Transcribing the Experts

Transcribing will serve several purposes in helping to:

1. Begin to perform what is first mentally conceived.
2. Propel the improviser's mind to adopt acceptable stylistic compositional choices.
3. Manifest the nuances of the composer.
4. Improve overall ear training for nonimprovisational situations.
5. Increase aural skills.

To truly understand the stylistic choices of an expert jazz musician like Miles Davis, it takes years of diligent study and analysis. With that said, we will take a small glimpse into how he approaches jazz and see if we can learn something by listening to him.

### Transcribe Exercise 1

First, listen to the tune "So What" from the album *Kind of Blue*. In his improvised solo, Miles is exceptional at playing clear, simple phrases. It is exceedingly clear how he takes little fragments or statements and builds upon them. In a sense, he improvises with himself. He plays a phrase and then takes that phrase and develops it. He then takes that developed phrase and develops it more intently. Therefore, he is able to play an interesting solo at great lengths without repeating himself.

Second, transcribe Miles Davis's improvised solo. Notice how Miles tends to play on the low side of the pitch. He also tends to lay back on the beat, so finding exactly where each beat lies may be difficult. Chances are, when you were transcribing his solo, you were more

102  *Crossing Over*

concerned with getting the right notes. This is good; however, now that you have all the right notes written down, it's time to put some style into it. The goal of transcribing is to be able to sound like Miles. Notice his inflections; there is more to style than just playing the right note. Jazz has a very distinct sound, and the best way to learn how to play in that style is to listen to people who know how to do it, like Miles. Notice his inflections and choices of which notes to emphasize with an accent and which notes not to emphasize. Notice his usage of half-valving, bending notes and how he lays back on the beat. These all make for a good jazz sound.

Once you memorize the notes, spend time listening to how he plays and not necessarily what he plays. You've probably listened to his solo numerous times, and you're sick of it by now. This is a good. What happens when you transcribe a solo is that, subliminally, you've heard Miles Davis play, which results in his style and phrasing burned into your subconscious. The real intention was for you to hear Miles a hundred times so that you'll be able to play in the correct style. Listening is the key to successfully playing in the jazz style.

To be clear, transcription is not about writing out the notes you hear on staff paper and then playing the notes by reading them on the page. Instead, this is an aural transcription. Listening and internalizing every aspect of what the expert performs on the recording by ear. It is about imitating the interpretative skills demonstrated by a professional performing artist.

### *Transcribe Exercise 2*

Record your own improvised solo on your instrument.
Listen back to the recording.
Sing along to the recording with only your voice.

### *Transcribe Exercise 3*

Sing an improvise solo and record it.
Listen back to the recording.
Transcribe the recording on your instrument.
Reminder: Do not write down any notes. This is all done by ear!

## Step 4: Avoiding Roadblocks

Stumbling blocks are circumstances that cause difficulty or hesitation. Every developing jazz improviser I have encountered in a lesson has, at one time or another, experienced some sort of roadblock between the desire to play something and the ability to produce it.

### *Drawing Blanks*

#### Roadblock—

A common roadblock for beginning improvisers is drawing a blank when it is their turn to improvise, whereby they are unable to play what they first conceive. This "deer in the headlights" experience is quite common among beginners. It is a mental state caused by fear, confusion, panic, or perhaps anxiety. A lack of experience, jazz vocabulary, technical facility, or perhaps a lack of confidence may cause fear, confusion, panic, or anxiety. Either way, drawing a blank when it is time to improvise is a common roadblock that is easy to fix.

### Solution—

Remember that jazz improvisation is like a language, and one must develop a stronger vocabulary in a language in order to have more involved conversations. There are several ways to combat the fear that prevents an improviser from playing what he hears first in his head. One way is to play what is known. Chances are, pieces that the beginning improviser works on will most likely be in a major key. Stick to playing melodies that have notes in the major scale of the key of the piece. Reinforcing the concepts discussed earlier in the book will also aid in the drawing-a-blank roadblock.

### Exercise—

Give yourself limits to what you are allowed to play. In this exercise, only play the notes in the Bb scale. Our main focus will be to focus on playing scales, practicing excellent voice leading. Continue by playing eighth notes only and for four bars. After the four bars, rest for two bars and then come in, only playing sixteenth notes—changing the parameters every four bars. This will limit your choices to help you better focus on knowing exactly what to play.

## Getting Lost

### Roadblock—

Getting lost, not knowing where one is while playing over changes, is another common roadblock. Following the chord changes while soloing may cause the improviser to lose focus and get lost in the progression. Don't worry so much about where you are; be concerned about what you are trying to say. Over time as you get more comfortable with your listening skills, you will be able to play your improvisations and line up with the chord changes.

### Solution—

Stop and listen. It is ok not to play all of the time—the bass player will outline the chord progression, and the drummer will more than likely help you by playing fills at the end of the progression and provide sonic devices to show you where the form is. Think about jazz improvisation as a group conversation, and you are only a part of the conversation, not the main speaker. Take the time to stop and listen to your surroundings and be a part of what you hear. Another solution is to ask for help. In jazz, it is ok to talk during a performance. I recommend that the improviser literally ask the question, "Where are we?" and most jazz musicians will provide the correct answer. Another solution is to know the sound of the piece. This is accomplished by listening to the chord progression multiple times.

### Exercise—

Play a track from any play-along audio recording, but start the track somewhere in the middle. Do not play. Just listen. Then when you think you hear where the beginning of the progression

104　*Crossing Over*

is, start your improvisation. Listen until you can recognize the changes, regardless of where the track is played, and without looking at a lead sheet.

### *Inability to Hear the Harmony*

**Roadblock—**

This roadblock connects to getting lost in the chord changes. Some improvisers have a hard time hearing the harmony. This is because they focus too much on responding to the changes without first listening to what the changes offer.

**Solution—**

Outline the chords. A solution to an improviser's inability to hear the harmony is to outline the chord progression of the piece performed. It is not enough to just listen to the chord changes; one must actively play through the changes in order to add another layer to one's understanding of the harmonic progression. If the improviser outlines the chords to the tune they are preparing, it will improve their ear and understanding of the harmony and provide forward momentum.

**Exercise—**

When outlining the chords, remember that the harmony is always moving. When playing chords, start with the root and play 1, 3, 5, 7 of each chord in quarter notes. Then do the same exercise on eighth notes, and then add other nonchord tones as passing tones. Try to outline each chord again, but this time start each chord on the third instead of the root. Change up the pattern as often as you'd like by starting on a new chord tone.

### *Having Too Many Ideas*

**Roadblock—**

Believe it or not, there is a chance that the beginning improviser may have too many ideas they will want to play. In this rare case, the beginning improviser will play many ideas in their solo, or perhaps they will just play many licks learned. This is a roadblock because a musician needs to learn that an improvised solo is an idea that gets developed and implemented within a larger conversation. Start to think about this now as you play your solo.

**Solution—**

If you find yourself playing a lot of ideas, or just playing licks, or that having too many ideas in your head causes nothing to come out, then there is a solution. Pick one idea and stick to it throughout the solo. Try to come up with a very simple melody that you can use to develop. A simple melody or one idea at a time is something to anchor to and also a good way to avoid getting lost.

*Playing Too Long*

**Roadblock—**

All too often, developing players play too many notes. Playing too many notes is like someone talking and rambling on and on. Think of improvisation as a conversation—a conversation with others or a conversation with yourself.

**Solution—**

Breathe. Play with intentional thought. Avoid playing just to play; think about what you want to say and then imagine what that would sound like through your instrument. Play what you hear, and then pause. The pause will allow time for you to think about exactly what you want to play next and will instill a sense of phrasing in your solos.

**Exercise—**

Two bars on, two bars off. Improvise for two bars, and then do not play for two bars. Then continue in the same manner, playing for two bars and resting for two bars. This exercise will help you play fewer notes and express your ideas in a more succinct, efficient way.

*Connecting One Chord to the Next*

**Roadblock—**

Once improvisers understand how to create a solo over one particular chord, say Bb, for example, they may have an issue playing over various chords. For example:

One Chord

Multiple Chords

**Solution/Exercise**

You are more than likely a half step away from the right note. Practice slowly in the transition between chord changes.

106    *Crossing Over*

To practice transitions between two different chords, stop at the last note of your phrase—in this case, it is an Ab in measure 4. Strive to learn to play the closest note from the last note (Ab) that will also fit in the new chord. You have a choice: from Ab you can play either a G or a Bb. This improviser chose G because it works in the new chord at measure 5 and is the closest note to Ab. Then from measure 5 to measure 6, it also happens to be an Ab to G. To connect measure 6 to measure 7, the improviser ended her phrase on a Bb and chose to play a half step lower to an A to connect to the next chord. Another strategy is to find the guide tone lines in the chord progression you are working on and use them as connecting points between bars.

### *Essential Elements Applied When Crossing Over*

### 1. Trust

Trust your ears will dictate what your body needs to do to create the desired sound.

### 2. Ability to Listen

Listen to as much jazz music as you do classical music.

### 3. Synergy

Synergize with the rest of the ensemble. The other members of the band will help engage in musical conversation.

### 4. Micromanagement and Macromanagement

Practicing in phrases will help cultivate a thought process on a *micro* level, connecting each phrase to achieve the goals of the *macro* level.

### 5. Realization

Realize that crossing over into something new involves a challenge that might get overwhelming. Try your best to look at the challenge, not as a stumbling block but something that gets you closer to what you desire.

### 6. Stepping into the Deep

Step into the deep by paying more attention to what you hear in your head and communicating your thoughts.

### 7. Confidence

Be confident in the fact that over time, the more you practice jazz, the more you will be better at it. The trick is to be patient and create complete ownership over the practiced concepts. According to Kenny Werner,

> While moving quickly through material, you're under the delusion that you are making progress. Spending enough time learning something would feel interminably slow, but that is the

way of true growth. It takes what it takes. The fact is that if you don't stay with the material long enough for it to become comfortable, you'll find that it doesn't stay with you . . . It really doesn't pay to move on until something is mastered.

And when something is mastered, improvisers become more confident in their ability to execute the desired technique at will.

## 8. Genuine Study of Craft

Study the steps. Remember to 1) conceptualize and transcribe, 2) simplify the melody, 3) start the melody with a chord tone, 4) avoid the tonic as a cadential point, 5) play "bad" notes on purpose and then resolve them, and 6) encircle a chord tone, playing notes to create tension on either side.

## 9. Practice

Do not overlook the importance of study and practice. If you want to cross over from an orchestral sound to a jazz sound, you must think like a jazz musician. You must learn to emulate a jazz musician's sound and train your playing to reflect a jazz sound. And when you do practice, (1) develop a sense of play and communication of ideas, (2) transcribe yourself with simple, singable melodies, (3) implement some rules to help focus your thoughts, (4) add style by transcribing the sound of an expert jazz linguist, and (5) as you progress, be aware of roadblocks and know there are solutions.

## 10. Imagination

Imagine what jazz players sound like, and emulate them. A great way to develop imagination is to transcribe professional jazz artists. Then as you are playing the notes you just transcribed, imagine that you are a player such as Miles Davis, Clifford Brown, Oscar Peterson, etc., and play the notes as they would play them.

*Select Jazz Recordings*
There is a tremendous amount of music to absorb when a musician learns to apply jazz to improvisation. Listen to as much jazz as possible. Listening will help develop vocabulary, expand musical nuance, and internalize melodic, harmonic, and rhythmic ideas. To be clear, this is not a definitive list of jazz recordings. This is a sample list of jazz recordings that will help you learn more about the language of jazz.

1. Fats Waller, "Handful of Keys" (Proper, 2004; tracks recorded 1922–43).
2. King Oliver, "King Oliver's Creole Jazz Band: The Complete Set" (Challenge, 1997; tracks recorded 1923).
3. Louis Armstrong, "The Complete Hot Five and Hot Seven Recordings" (Sony, 2006; tracks recorded 1925–29).
4. Louis Armstrong, "The Complete RCA Victor Recordings" (RCA, 2001; tracks recorded 1932–33 and 1946–47).
5. Louis Armstrong, "Louis Armstrong Plays W. C. Handy" (Columbia, 1954).
6. Bessie Smith, "The Essential Bessie Smith" (Sony, 1997; tracks recorded 1923–33).

108 *Crossing Over*

7. Django Reinhardt, "The Classic Early Recordings in Chronological Order" (JSP, 2000; tracks recorded 1934–39).
8. Jelly Roll Morton, "Jelly Roll Morton: 1926–1930" (JSP, 2000).
9. Jelly Roll Morton: The Complete Library of Congress Recordings (Rounder Records, 2005)
10. Duke Ellington, "Ellington at Newport 1956" (Sony, 1999).
11. Duke Ellington, "Money Jungle" (Blue Note Records, 1962).
12. Coleman Hawkins, "The Bebop Years" (Proper, 2001; tracks recorded 1939–49).
13. Lester Young, "Kansas City Swing" (Definitive, 2004; tracks recorded 1938–44).
14. Count Basie, "The Complete Decca Recordings" (Verve, 1992; tracks recorded 1937–39).
15. Benny Goodman, "At Carnegie Hall—1938—Complete" (Columbia, 1999).
16. Charlie Parker, "Bird: The Complete Charlie Parker on Verve" (Polygram, 1988; tracks recorded 1946–54).
17. Charlie Parker, "Best of the Complete Live Performances on Savoy" (Savoy, 2002; tracks recorded 1948–49).
18. Dizzy Gillespie and Charlie Parker, "Town Hall, New York City, June 22, 1945" (Uptown Jazz, 2005).
19. Dizzy Gillespie, "The Complete RCA Victor Recordings, 1947–49" (RCA, 1995).
20. Thelonious Monk, "Genius of Modern Music, Vol. 1" (Blue Note, 2001; tracks recorded 1947).
21. Thelonious Monk, "Thelonious Monk with John Coltrane: The Complete 1957 Riverside Recordings" (Riverside, 2006).
22. Miles Davis, "The Complete Birth of the Cool" (Blue Note, 1998; tracks recorded 1948–50).
23. Miles Davis, "Kind of Blue" (Sony, 1959).
24. Gerry Mulligan, "The Original Quartet with Chet Baker" (Blue Note, 1998; tracks recorded 1952–53).
25. Modern Jazz Quartet, "Django" (Prestige, 1953).
26. Clifford Brown and Max Roach, "Clifford Brown & Max Roach" (EmArcy, 1954).
27. Charles Mingus, "Mingus Ah Um" (Columbia, 1959).
28. Sonny Rollins, "Saxophone Colossus" (Prestige, 1956).
29. Sonny Rollins, "Night at the Village Vanguard" (Blue Note, 1957).
30. Art Blakey and the Jazz Messengers, "Moanin'" (Blue Note, 1958).
31. John Coltrane, "My Favorite Things" (Atlantic, 1960).
32. Clifford Brown: "Clifford Brown and Max Roach" (EmArcy, 1954)
33. John Coltrane, "The Complete 1961 Village Vanguard Recordings" (GRP, 1997; tracks recorded 1961).
34. John Coltrane, "A Love Supreme" (Impulse!, 1964).
35. Bill Evans, "The Complete Village Vanguard Recordings, 1961" (Riverside, 2005).
36. Stan Getz and João Gilberto, "Getz/Gilberto" (Verve, 1963).
37. Lee Morgan, "The Sidewinder" (Blue Note, 1963).
38. Frank Sinatra, "Sinatra at the Sands with Count Basie & the Orchestra" (Reprise, 1966).
39. Frank Sinatra, "The Capitol Years" (Capitol, 1990; tracks recorded 1953–62).
40. Chick Corea, "Return to Forever" (ECM, 1972).
41. Keith Jarrett, "The Köln Concert, 1975" (ECM, 1999).
42. Wynton Marsalis Septet, "Live at the Village Vanguard" (Sony, 1999).
43. Ornette Coleman: *The Shape of Jazz to Come* (Atlantic, 1959)

44. Dave Brubeck: *Time Out* (Columbia, 1959)
45. John Coltrane: *Giant Steps* (Atlantic, 1960)
46. Oscar Peterson: *Night Train* (Verve, 1963)
47. Herbie Hancock: *Head Hunters* (Columbia, 1973)
48. Hank Mobley: *Soul Station* (Blue Note, 1960)
49. Charlie Parker: *Charlie Parker with Strings* (Mercury, 1950)
50. Clifford Brown: "Study in Brown" (EmArcy Records, 1955)

# 10 Classical Language for the Jazz Improviser

## An Introduction to Terms for Western Art Music Improvisation

As a young improviser studying jazz, I felt confident that, with analysis and practice, I would be able to apply lessons learned and express the right style within a given piece. This was partly due to the accessibility of authentic recordings that expressed specific stylistic nuances of a particular jazz style. With a plethora of recordings at my disposal, it was evident in the early stages of my development whether or not I was able, in my improvisation, to represent the style in the most accurate way, that is, adding too much Clifford Brown when playing late 19th century traditional New Orleans music. Can the same be said about early Western European improvisation? How can musicians express the nuances of pre-romantic period improv in the most accurate and authentic way? Does the act of improvising in early music today misrepresent the music?

I've mentioned earlier how I believe those who play by ear as opposed to first learning what scale works with a certain chord have an advantage. However, there are no known recordings of music made before the 19th century. Therefore, the best way to learn is to examine the surviving written music and study the pedagogical tradition.

There has been much scholarship in understanding the classical language, as evident in the list of resources compiled in this book. This chapter does not attempt to provide a comprehensive exploration of historical performance practice. It means to give the musicians a brief background and context for entry-level awareness of various improvised Western art music. The context and background explored in this chapter will prepare musicians for a more in-depth study of their chosen genre and prepare them for exercises in the next chapter. Sample topics in this chapter include aspects of medieval music, Renaissance music, Baroque music, classical period cadenzas, and atonal free improvisation.

### An Entry Level Introduction to Medieval Music Terminology

Musicologists can categorize music most associated with the medieval period as appearing from c450–c1450. One of the earliest types of music in this time period was chant. Chant is monophonic Christian (typically Roman Catholic) music in free rhythm. While most music can be connected to the church (liturgical music), other nonliturgical music existed in this period. For example, nonliturgical monophony by French troubadours thrived in the 12th century (*Concise History of Western Music*, Hanning 2014). This music consisted of a single melodic line with or without accompaniment.

Throughout the period, music evolved from monophonic textures to polyphonic textures. An early form of polyphony is known as organum. According to the *New Harvard Dictionary*

DOI:10.4324/9781003341857-10

*of Music*, the word organum means tool or instrument. How it came to be associated with polyphony is not entirely clear. According to the new *New Harvard Dictionary of Music*, the most persuasive of several explanations suggested thus far finds the key in the adjectival form *organicus*, a term commonly used to describe the precise measurement of pitches or intervals. As polyphonic music developed, we see the rise of the motet, a major musical genre first appearing in the 13th century. (*Concise History of Western Music*, Hanning 2014). The definition of a motet depends on the time frame. In the medieval period, the term denoted a particular structure. According to the *New Harvard Dictionary of Music*, the structure involved a tenor line derived from chant that serves as the foundation for new composed upper voices. Motet was considered a genre or "polyphonic setting of a sacred Latin text." After 1600, the term became associated with a particular style. The style is "the serious, imitative style of church polyphony derived from Palestrina."

## An Entry Level Introduction to Renaissance Music Terminology

The expectation of musicians throughout the Renaissance was to improvise new material as well as read the composed material. (Stolba 1994) From the mid-1530s to 1600, professional musicians wrote treatises to provide instruction on how to improvise. While each version may have had its own take on the rules governing improvisation, given the region and nature of a particular instrument or voice, all made it clear that ornamentation was commonplace (Atlas 1998). According to Maria Stolba, performers usually improvised in one of three ways:

1. By adding one or more new polyphonic lines to an existing melody selected as cantus firmus.
2. By embellishing or paraphrasing an existing melody.
3. By freely improvising, without reference to a preexistent melody or harmony or predetermined formal pattern.

Throughout this period, many composer-performers were writing their own versions of how to use ornaments. Their texts, or treatises, taught readers how to play the music of this time period.

Using ornaments was a way to decorate existing melodies. The three different categories of ornaments, according to Allan Atlas, are

1. embellishments for single notes,
2. decorations that fill in intervals between notes, and
3. ornamented versions of the top voice part of entire compositions.

If you are interested in learning more in-depth about this music, I recommend reading any of the texts provided at the end of this chapter. As an example, take Aurelio Virgiliano's manuscript *Il Dolcimelo*, and look at some of the "rules" that could help the beginner get started:

1. Any division notes that leap must be consonant.
2. Try to play up to the octave or down to the octave.
3. The written note must be played at the beginning, middle, and end. If you can't play the original note in the middle of the measure, it is best to play a chord tone instead of a dissonant note.
4. When a division leaps, it should leap to a chord tone and not a dissonant note.
5. Play in a stepwise fashion.

112  *Classical Language for the Jazz Improviser*

Ground bass in this time period is similar to a twelve-bar blues. It was a harmonic practice that involved a bass line that repeated. The repeated bass line formed a harmonic chord progression. Examples of this type of Renaissance form include folia and canarios. For the Baroque period, it would include chaconne and passacaglia.

## An Entry Level Introduction to Baroque Music Terminology

Much like the Renaissance Period, a number of published treatises came to the fore during the 17th and 18th centuries. According to Barbara Hanning, most treatises were written for a specific instrument, such as lute or keyboard, and tailored to the tastes of a certain region. She goes on to say that one of the most important treatises in France was L'Art de toucher le clavecin (*The Art of Playing the Harpsichord*, 1716) by Francois Couperin. While this chapter will not dive deeply into all of the "rules" to perform Baroque music, a novice improviser needs to understand some basic terminology associated with improvisation throughout this time frame. According to the *New Harvard Dictionary of Music*, the following terms are defined as the following:

> *Fugue* is the most fully developed procedure of imitative counterpoint. The theme is stated successively in all voices of the polyphonic texture, tonally established, continuously expanded, opposed, and reestablished.
>
> *Figured Bass*, also known as basso continuo, is a method for harmonic notation originating in the Baroque era. Instead of writing modern chord symbols, a composer would provide a bass line with marks below to specify which intervals above that base note are acceptable within the harmony.

## An Entry Level Introduction to Cadenzas, Variations, and Prologue Music Terminology

### Improvised Cadenza

The form of a concerto composed by J.C. Bach in the classical period involves a ritornello (orchestral exposition), then a solo (solo exposition), and then another ritornello. Another solo follows, but this time in development, then a brief orchestral cadence, then a recapitulation of the solo section with a cadenza closing with a final ritornello section. According to Barbara Hanning, by Bach's time, it had become traditional for the soloist to play an improvised cadenza just before the final orchestral ritornello. According to Robert Levin, the artificial pause by the orchestra becomes a springboard for improvisation because it is a moment of dissonance that needs to resolve. This moment of dissonance is the I 6/4 chord. Levin suggests that the goal is to provide an inventive peroration that will end by concluding the formula, which will then precipitate the reentry of the orchestra. Tunes from the body of the concerto, Levin ascertains, can be invoked and developed, but that is less critical than carrying out the harmonic tension throughout that final trill.

### Variations

Robert Levin has said improvising variations on a familiar theme was one of the staples of a public concert—sometimes a composer like Mozart would do it on his own, but more often on popular arias of the time. The goal of an improviser in variations is to alter the properties of the theme while keeping it recognizable.

### *Prologue Music*

Think of this type of music as giving the listener information that will help them comprehend the piece that follows. Much like a prologue in a work of written fiction, this could include character backstory or information that establishes the story's backdrop. I use the term *prologue music* to encompass all the different types of freely improvised music that occurred before longer, more involved works. These improvised works include music such as intonations, toccatas, fantasias, ricercars, and preludes fall into this category. According to Claude Palisca, these types of freely improvised forms arose from the following: 1) a musician's need to tune his instrument, 2) set the tonality for a vocal performance, 3) warm up the improviser's technique, 4) provide entry music for stage performers or other musicians, or 5) occasionally fill an interlude between songs and dances.

### An Entry Level Introduction to Aleatoric Music and Free Improvisation Terminology

According to the *New Harvard Dictionary of Music*, aleatory music is 20th century music in which deliberate use is made of chance or indeterminacy. In this type of music, composers utilize a random process to determine aspects of the composition, or the performer makes certain compositional decisions within a conceived piece. Derek Bailey said that

> freely improvised music, variously called 'total improvisation,' 'open improvisation,' 'free music,' or perhaps most often simply, 'improvised music,' suffers from—and enjoys—the confused identity which its resistance to labeling indicates. It is a logical situation: freely improvised music is an activity which encompasses too many different concepts of what improvisation is, even, for it all to be subsumed under one name.

He goes on to say,

> Diversity is its most consistent characteristic. It has no stylistic or idiomatic commitment. It has no prescribed idiomatic sound. The characteristics of freely improvised music are established only by the sonic musical identity of the person or persons playing it.

### *Other Sources*

Here is a list of sources for further study of genre-specific historically accurate applications:

*A Performer's Guide to Seventeenth Century Music*, Stewart Carter
Indiana University Press, 2012

*Renaissance Music*, Allan W. Atlas
W.W. Norton & Company, Inc, 1998

*A Performer's Guide to Medieval Music*, Ross W. Duffin
Indiana University Press, 2002

*A Performer's Guide to Renaissance Music*, Jeffery Kite-Powell
Indiana University Press, 2007

*Baroque Music: Style and Performance: A Handbook*, Robert Donington
W.W. Norton, 1982

*The Interpretation of Music*, Robert Donington
W.W. Norton, 1963

*The Art of Partimento: History, Theory, and Practice*, G. Sanguinetti
Oxford University Press, 2012

*Improvisation and Inventio in the Performance of Medieval Music: A Practical Approach*, Angela
    Mariani, Oxford University Press, 2017.

*The Performance of 16th Century Music: Learning from the Theorists*, Anne Smith
Oxford University Press, 2011

*The Art of Accompaniment from a Thorough-Bass*, F.T. Arnold
Dover Publications, 2003

*On Playing the Flute*, Johann Joachim Quantz
Northeastern University Press, 2001

*Treatise on the Ornaments of Music*, Giuseppe Tartini
Carl Fischer, 1960

*Classical and Romantic Performing Practice*, Clive Brown
Oxford University Press, 1999

*Il Dolcimelo*, Aurelio Virgiliano, ca. 1600
Reprint Anne Fuzeau Productions, 2001.

*L'art de toucher le clavecin*, Francois Couperin 1716

### *Essential Elements For Understanding Classical Language*

### 1. Trust

Trust that the classical language is like any other language. It takes time to learn and develop.
Several treaties clearly outline precise ways to interpret the music of that time period and region.
I would recommend Quantz's *On the Playing of the Flute*, Tartini's *Treatise on the Ornaments of
Music*, Couperin's *L'art de toucher le clavecin*, and Virgiliano's *Il Dolcimelo*.

### 2. Ability to Listen

While listening to authentic recordings from the time period is impossible, listening to
scholar-performers interpret early music is possible. These scholar-performers are the closest

we have to authentic recordings of early Western music. I strongly recommend to seek out as many recordings as possible to hear how these performers interpret the style and nuance of this early material. Some excellent performers include Bruce Dickey, Adam Gilbert, Trevor Pinnock, John Eliot Gardiner, Christopher Hogwood, Emmanuelle Haim, William Christie, Rene Jacobs, Giardino Armonico, Leonardo Alarcon, Jaap Schroeder, Rachel Podger, Ton Koopman, Franz Bruggen, Jordi Savall, Roger Norrington, David Munrow, Musica Antiqua Köln, Orchestra of the Eighteenth Century, Ensemble Solazzo, Piffaro, Ciarmella, Baltimore Consort, Dark Horse Consort, Ensemble Micrologus, Early Music New York, and Waverly Consort.

## 3. Synergy

The collaboration between musicians in the classical idiom is just as vital to successful performances as it is in the jazz idiom. Improvisers are always synergizing their roles to create something bigger than themselves.

## 4. Micromanagement and Macromanagement

Think about utilizing ornaments on both the micro and macro levels. While numerous rules should be employed when applying the right style to a particular piece, it is also just as important to consider how to both micro and macromanage your improvisation. On the micro level, think about all of the rules needed for historically accurate performance and apply them as needed. At the same time, think about how those ornaments fulfill the larger intent and direction of the piece on the macro level.

## 5. Realization

To understand the classical language, musicians must realize that there is an expectation to improvise within this style. It is important for those interested in this type of music to seek out further reading of treatises and published texts on early music performance practice.

## 6. Stepping into the Deep

Once you obtain a moderate level of proficiency in applying the concept of intention to invention in the non-jazz style, I would encourage you to seek out authentic period instruments for practice and performance. Step into the deep of instruments such as the cornetto, sackbut, shawm, viola de gamba, lute, crumhorn, recorder, dulcian, natural trumpet, harpsichord, and viola de gamba, etc. Improvising on period instruments will give musicians yet another layer of understanding this style.

## 7. Confidence

When first learning to decode the classical language, it is perfectly natural to feel apprehensive. Most beginning improvisers could become overwhelmed when introduced to the massive number of rules. As musicians work on decoding the language, they need to have the confidence to know that once they learn the rules, improvising in this style becomes gradually easier to execute in the moment.

## 8. Genuine Study of Craft

Improvisers must study the basic terms associated with the various time periods. Knowing the terms will help provide context when practicing the concepts needed to execute historically accurate improvisations.

## 9. Practice

There will be a series of exercises to help garner skills to improvise in this style in the next chapter. Learning to apply improvisation to a particular style, such as Baroque music, takes time. There is no substitute for practicing intention, invention, and application specific to the desired style each day.

## 10. Imagination

In addition to learning the rules and daily applied practice, it is important to remind yourself of the purpose of this music. Imagine yourself in the 17th century as a court musician playing for a dance. What are the movements of the dance? How slow? How fast? Using your imagination will add another layer of artistic depth to your improvisation.

# 11 Improvisation Exercises Inspired by Classical Genres

Improvisers need to understand that "classical" improvisation is just as demanding as jazz. In my experience improvising in both jazz and classical forms of music, the most significant difference is the sound concept. Quite frankly, even within jazz or classical music itself, there are different sound concepts I attempt to create. For example, in jazz, if I am improvising a solo within a piece centered in New Orleans around the early 20th century, I want to project a sound that represents something close to Louis Armstrong. However, if I am attempting to play a tune such as "You Made Me Love You" in the 1940s, I will want to project a sound concept similar to that of Harry James instead. For "classical" music, the improviser needs to make the same sort of distinctions in character. For each time period of early music, in addition to following several rules, there were certain characteristics of sound. For example, when I improvise a melody based on a Baroque saraband, I will want to apply a stately character, dance-like, and triple meter to maintain the correct style. So how can improvisers begin the process of applying the intention to invention process to genres that fall under the classical umbrella? How can one convey an artistic idea through "classical" language but in real time? Are there exercises that help introduce this language to a beginner?

**Monophonic Exercise**

This monophonic exercise will incorporate aspects of chant. Remember that chant is a musical texture consisting of a single unaccompanied melodic line in free rhythm. The soloist should

1. begin by using one of the church modes—for example, the Dorian mode,
2. limit self to only using notes within one octave,
3. create a mysterious character and avoid a sense of meter or time,
4. create a vocal quality and imagine the elongation of vowels, and
5. at first, if using D Dorian, start and end with D.

Dorian Mode

Improvised Chant using Dorian Example

Notice in this example that the improvised chant is monophonic and void of a strict meter or rhythmic pulse. This example begins and ends with D and is limited to only using notes within one octave. Try to use these limitations when creating your own improvised chant. Now it is your turn.

- Avoid bar lines and note stems to create free rhythm.
- Make sure the chant is stepwise with minimal large leaps within one octave.
- Think about a sense of cadence by elongating some notes.
- Try to keep your phrases short.
- Explore the idea of cadencing on different notes instead of the same note.

**Polyphonic Exercises**

This polyphonic exercise will incorporate aspects of organum. This exercise involves at least two improvisers. Improviser 1 begins by improvising a cantus firmus. A good place to start would be to create a simple, short, and singable chant. Before the second improviser comes in, make sure that Improviser 1 can replicate what he played multiple times. This will allow Improviser 1 the opportunity to make sure what he heard mentally was projected through his instrument and to enable Improviser 2 the chance to improvise a new melody to create a polyphonic texture. For advanced players, have Improviser 2 improvise his part simultaneously as Improviser 1 without hearing Improviser 1 perform first. There are three versions of this exercise.

*Version 1: Rhythmic*

In this version, begin with the first player improvising a main chant melody. As Improviser 1 plays the main melody, Improviser 2 performs the same rhythm yet stays on one note. Improviser 1 must project confidence and clarity in shaping the melody. Improviser 2 must listen intently to the direction of Improviser 1.

*Version 2: Parallel*

In this version, begin with the first player improvising a main chant melody. Improviser 2 performs the same melody a fifth apart from one another. The challenge for Improviser 2 is to listen to the rhythmic quality of Improviser 1. Additionally, Improviser 2 must listen to the direction of the pitches and be able to match the contour a fifth a part from the original line.

## Version 3: Free

In this final version, begin with the first player improvising a main chant melody. Similar to the previous two versions, Improviser 2 should perform the same rhythm as Improviser 1. However, parallel motion and contrary motion can occur between both improvisers.

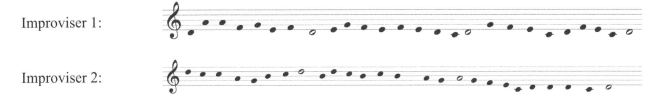

Improviser 1:

Improviser 2:

## Form Exercise

The various forms inspiring this exercise include binary, ternary, rondo, sonata. Use these exercises to help develop a better sense of form within music.

### Simple Binary (A, B)

This musical form is divided into two sections that contrast with each other. The contrast could be a new key, melodic material or harmonic material. For example, the A section could be in the tonic, then the B section could be in the dominant. Another example could be the A section is in D minor and B section is in F major, the relative major.

- Begin by improvising a melody over the course of four bars (a section). This melody should be kept simple and singable.
- After this, improvise a new melody over the course of another four bars (b).

Remember that this is all done by ear! Listen to the melody you create in your head, and transcribe that melody through your instrument.

Please note: There are variations of binary such as AA$^1$. As an introduction, I suggest focusing your attention on simple AB form. In this example, I've improvised a four-bar melody in C major for the A section. Then to create contrast in the B section, I've improvised a four-bar melody in A minor.

### Rounded Binary (A, B, A)

This type of form is similar to binary and is a great transition step toward learning ternary form. Rounded binary has an A Section followed by a B section. Then after the B Section, play a little bit of the original A Section.

120    *Improvisation Exercises Inspired by Classical Genres*

- Begin by improvising a melody over the course of four bars (A section). This melody should be kept simple and singable.
- After this, improvise a new melody over the course of another four bars (A).
- Finally, perform two bars of the original A section.

Remember that this is all done by ear! Listen to the melody you create in your head, and transcribe that melody through your instrument.

To give you an idea of what rounded binary sounds like, here is an example of Mozart's Allegro fur das Pianoforte K. No. 3. (1762). Use this as an example to get an idea of the sound of this type of binary. Your improvisation inspired by this form should be kept simple, singable, and short. As you develop, the form can increase in size and scope.

### Ternary (A, B, A)

This is a musical structure where the improvisation is divided into three sections. To end each section, use a perfect authentic cadence. Think of a perfect authentic cadence as a tonic chord in root position with the tonic note in both the bass and the soprano line. This cadence will help make each part (A and B) sound complete and not sound as if it should continue to the next section. Regarding how each section should contrast one another, the same rules apply here as they did in binary form.

- Begin by improvising a melody over the course of four bars (A section). This melody should be kept simple and singable ending with a perfect authentic cadence.
- After four bars, improvise a four-bar contrasting melody (B section). This melody should be kept simple and singable, ending with a perfect authentic cadence.
- Go back and repeat the same improvised melody from the original a section (A Section).

Using the previous improvisation in simple binary, notice how I have added a fully restated A Section. Also, notice that in measures 4 and in measure 8, the cadence is a perfect authentic cadence to provide a clear distinction between sections.

### Rondo Form (Five Part: A, B, A, C, A—Seven Part: A, B, A, C, A, B, A)

Think of this as theme and variation, but the theme always comes back! The main theme (A section) alternates with contrasting themes (B, C, etc). Each new section must contrast in some way to the previous material. As in the previous forms, the contrast could be melodic, harmonic, key relationship, etc. When improvising your melodies, try to keep this in mind:

- The A section is in tonic.
- The B section could be in a closely related key.
- The C section uses a larger variety of keys.
- To start, predetermine the length of each section and the chords associated with each section.

As a reminder, this exercise is to help develop a better sense of form within music. This is not an approach to an in-depth study of Rondo form. The idea is for the improviser to be thinking in both the present moment (creating melodies within a section) and thinking about future moments (creating melodies in the next section that contrast to the main A theme). Remember that this is all done by ear! Listen to the melody you create in your head, and transcribe that melody through your instrument. Keep melodies simple and singable.

To start: Try using this harmonic formula as a basis to hear your melodies

| Five-Part Rondo Formula | C Major Five-Part Rondo Example |
|---|---|
| • A Section: I<br>• B Section: V<br>• A Section: I<br>• C Section: vi<br>• A Section: I | • A Section: C<br>• B Section: G<br>• A Section: C<br>• C Section: A minor<br>• A Section: C |

**Style Exercises**

In addition to being able to see opportunities to embellish a melody, the improviser needs to be able to sound like a musician from the Western European early music period (c. 1550–1750)

As discussed in the previous chapter, authentic recordings from the time period are not available. However, if improvisers are ready to apply style to their improvisations, I would recommend checking out some of my favorite texts on this topic.

---

**Texts to Help Apply Style**

Johann Joachim Quantz—*On Playing the Flute*
Giuseppe Tartini—*Treatise on the Ornaments of Music*
Aurelio Virgiliano—*Il Dolcimelo*
Francois Couperin—*L'art de toucher le clavecin*

---

These texts written by composers of the time period give their opinions on correctly applying the right ornament in the correct style within a composition. Don't let the titles deter you from reading them. For example, Quantz's text, while focusing on the flute, is really informative for all players. Similarly with Couperin's text, while it may focus on the keyboard, there is a lot of helpful information for all musicians.

Also, to be clear, Virgiliano's treatise is from 1600, while Couperin's *L'art de toucher* is from 1716. A lot happened in that century, so do not try to use Virgiliano to inform your improvisations on Bach or Handel. Instead, use Virgiliano, for example, as a way to help the beginner improvisor learn how to apply style. For the sake of learning how to apply style to the intention/invention process, I would recommend to choose one of these texts, then pick four or five suggestions, and exercise those suggestions until they are ingrained.

---

**Apply "the Rules"**

Choose a text.
Choose four or five suggestions within the chosen text.
Practice only those suggestions until the body and mind condition themselves.

---

First: Choose a text. How about Viirgiliano's *Il Dolcimelo*?
Second: Choose four or five "rules."

1) Try to play up to the octave or down to the octave.
2) Musicians must play the written note at the beginning, middle, and end. If a musician can't play the original note in the middle of the measure, then it is best to play a chord tone and not a dissonant note.
3) When a division leaps, it should leap to a chord tone and not a dissonant note.
4) Play, for the most part, in a stepwise fashion.

Third: Take your time, and only practice using these "rules" when embellishing the following melodic line. This style of exercise will incorporate aspects of early Western European dance music. The following melodies are inspired by music from the Renaissance and Baroque periods.

Melody 1

Melody 2

Melody 3

## Melodic Exercises

The study of ornamentation in the early music period can lead an improviser down a rabbit hole of information. This chapter, in particular, means to provide a springboard to help beginners start down this educational road and focus their minds better when learning more in-depth materials. The goal of these melodic exercises will incorporate aspects of ground bass.

While there are many forms and styles of grounds throughout Western Europe pre-1900, begin by choosing one and working on improvising melodies and variations of that melody over one set of chords/bass line. Use the lessons from previous chapters on how to create melodies and improvise over the following:

## Folia

*Example of improvised melody*

## Canon

*Example of improvised melody*

## Descending Bass Line

*Example of improvised melody*

When you improvise over these chord progressions, try to think about creating melodies in three different ways: 1. *melodic* using florid passages and linear stepwise contour; 2. *harmonic*—melodically outlining the arpeggio and creating tension with non-chord tones, then resolving that tension; 3. *rhythmic*—creating melodies with a focus on a variety of rhythmic variation.

**Harmony Exercise**

This harmony exercise will incorporate aspects of figured bass and is geared more toward beginning improvisers. The most important part of this exercise is to learn the "figured bass code." This code is a way to help introduce the concept to beginning improvisers as a precursor to more advanced study. Think of this code as a helpful tool to harmonize a particular note.

Understand the code:

No number = a triad chord
5/3 = a triad chord
6/3 = a triad in first inversion
6 = a triad in first inversion
6/4 = a triad in second inversion
4 = a triad chord in root position, but replace the 3 above the bass with a 4
7 = a seventh chord in root position
6/5 = a seventh chord in first inversion
4/3 = a seventh chord in second inversion
4/2 = a seventh chord in third inversion
Accidental next to a number = apply that accidental to the interval above the bass
A slash through a number, a plus sign next to a number = raise that note by one half step
Accidental only (no number) = the accidental is placed on the third above the bass
If there are numbers underneath a half or whole note, the harmony moves while the bass stays the same.
If there is a note in the bass that lands on the offbeat, do not realize this note.

See figured bass example:

See realized figured bass example:

128  *Improvisation Exercises Inspired by Classical Genres*

Using the provided bass line, improvise the harmony. The markings below the bass line indicate which intervals above that bass note are acceptable within that harmony. Keep transitions smooth and relatively within the same area of the keyboard (if playing keyboard) until there is a cadence.

### *Level 1: One Musician*

In this exercise, multi-note players such as keyboard and guitar read the figured bass notation and improvise as directed.

### *Level 2: Multiple Musicians*

Use the same figured bass examples. However, in this exercise, one musician plays the printed bass line, another musician realizes the figured bass, and the third musician improvises his own or embroiders the printed melody.

1.

Improvisation Exercises Inspired by Classical Genres 129

130 *Improvisation Exercises Inspired by Classical Genres*

10.

## Fugue-ish Exercise I

The goal for this exercise is to create a fugue-like composition in real time using four improvisers. This entry level exercise does not follow the typical structure of a fugue; instead, it helps create an improvisatorial nature for the group to learn ensemble listening skills and explore ways to develop a theme. Each improviser has a specific role, and each musical line has a specific time as to when to enter, when to develop, and when to end. Learners can do this exercise with multiple players in an ensemble or a single musician playing a multi-note instrument such as a piano or organ.

### *Theme*

Improviser 1 performs a musical line that is clearly defined. The main melody of this musical line needs to be simple enough for other improvisers to understand and quickly be able to play back easily.

### *Theme and Developed Theme*

Once Improviser 1 completes his theme, Improviser 2 plays the same melodic line. As Improviser 2 plays the main melodic line, Improviser 1 develops the main melody, creating a polyphonic texture.

132  *Improvisation Exercises Inspired by Classical Genres*

*Theme and Two Developed Themes*

Once Improviser 2 completes the main melodic theme and begins developing it, Improviser 3 enters and plays the main melodic theme.

*Theme and Three Developed Themes*

Once Improviser 3 completes the main melodic theme and begins developing it, Improviser 4 enters and plays the main melodic theme. At this point, Improviser 4 plays the main melody, and the other three improvisers improvise alternative melodies that counterpoint to the main melody.

## Development Section

Once Improviser 4 completes the final statement of the subject, and all improvisers are playing alternative melodies to the main idea, the exposition is over. From this point, all improvisers are developing the melody, then in sequential order, have each improviser restate the main original theme. When the fourth improviser finishes restating the main original theme, all players should play an ending.

## Ending

The exercise is over when Improviser 4 decides to present the main thematic subject in its original form after the development section and after the other three improvisers have restated the theme. The other improvisers must listen for this and drive their lines to an end resolution.

For Fugue Exercise #1, the idea is to create a fugue-like composition where each improviser listens and reacts to each other, as opposed to the goal of Fugue Exercise #2, which is to create a thoroughly composed fugue involving subject-answer relationships in new keys, episodes in retrograde motion, or inversion, etc.

## Fugue Exercise #2

The goal for this group exercise is to create a fugue in real time using four improvisers. Each improviser has a specific role, and each musical line has a specific time as to when to enter, when to develop, and when to end. Please note that this exercise may be a bit perplexing for the beginner. Use this exercise to help the advanced students in need of a challenge.

## Subject

Improviser 1 improvises the main theme or subject. For the sake of the exercise, the main theme needs to be simple enough for other improvisers to understand and quickly be able to play back easily.

## Subject and Answer

Once the main theme created by Improviser 1 is complete, Improviser 2 plays the same theme but up a fifth starting on the dominant, known as the answer. As Improviser 2 plays the answer, Improviser 1 develops the main melody in counterpoint to Improviser 2. This is known as the countersubject, thus creating a polyphonic texture.

### Third Improviser Entry

Once Improviser 2 completes the answer and begins developing it, Improviser 3 enters and plays the main theme either up or down the octave from the original.

### The Exposition

Once Improviser 3 completes the main theme and begins developing it, Improviser 4 enters and plays an answer to Improviser 3. At this point, when all voices have entered, this ends what is known as the exposition and begins the development section.

## Development Section

Similar to Fugue Exercise 1, in this section, improvisers can use several tools such as diminution, augmentation, inversion, and canon to develop the main theme. From this point, all improvisers are developing the melody, then in sequential order, have each improviser restate the main original theme. By the time the fourth improviser finishes restating the main original theme, all musicians should play an ending.

## Ending

The exercise is over when Improviser 4 decides to present the main thematic subject in its original form one last time. The other improvisers must listen for this and drive their lines to an end resolution.

## Cadenza Exercise

Years ago, when I first studied classical concertos, I wanted to challenge myself by improvising my cadenzas instead of performing pre-written ones. My enthusiasm was quickly brought down once I hit the practice room and realized how challenging this endeavor would be. The biggest hurdle for me then was where to start. As an educator, I encourage students who want to begin the process of improvising their cadenzas to focus their attention on the main themes of the movement.

Think of a soloist who improvises a cadenza as you would an improvisational comedic actor. An improv actor may take a suggestion from an audience and then create a scene about that suggestion. The audience predetermines the suggestion. However, the actor decides the direction of where to take the audience's input. Similar to this example, a musician improvising a cadenza uses melodic material from the piece as a resource to develop her own composition. While the themes and style have been determined within the piece (the suggestion), it is up to the improviser to create something that expresses her technical and musical ability, all while utilizing the composer's style. I recommend seeking out the main melody or principal themes. The theme or main melody of the piece is valuable material to use as a tool to create while being anchored by the parameters set by the composer. The point of the exercises is to provide musicians with tools to use to help apply the intention to invention process to cadenzas. For more information about style, I would recommend checking out works authored by Robert Levin.

### *Level 1: Melody*

Think of this three-note melody as the suggestion.

*Example: Three Note Ascension: A fictional work composed by J.P. Finch*

Take the suggestion and invent fresh material to create a new, improvised melody. Reshaping the existing material will help the improviser maintain the composer's intent while having the freedom to express her voice. Experiment with the following choices:

Choice 1: Adding a new note at rests (adding an F half note, keep the same rhythm)

Choice 2: Adding a new rhythm (keeping the same notes but changing the rhythm)

Choice 3: Adding a new note with a new rhythm

Choice 4: Adding passing or neighboring tones

Choice 5: Chromaticism

Choice 6: Arpeggiate

Choice 7: Augmentation

Choice 8: Diminution

Choice 9: Create intervals (such as adding a note between the three-note phrase)

**Level 2: Melody, Form**

Once there is a moderate comfort level with altering the main themes of the movement to help improvise a cadenza, the next step is to think about form. Try this:

1. Play the main theme.
2. Develop the main theme.
3. Play the second theme.
4. Develop the second theme.
5. Create a coda.
6. Trill on a V chord and resolve.

138  *Improvisation Exercises Inspired by Classical Genres*

### *Level 3: Melody, Harmony, Form*

Concepts to think about for level three:

- Think about improvising cadenzas as embellishing a final cadence—a sort of prolonged dominant chord (I64 to V).
- Maintain an overall sense of the prevailing key of the concerto.
- Try not to modulate into distant keys.
- Match the character of the particular concerto.
- Explore sequences, altered themes, virtuosic runs, passages in thirds.

In the first two levels of this exercise, the improviser focuses on altering the melody and experimenting with form. This level incorporates melody, form, and harmony. As an exercise to help apply the intention to invention process, try the Three Section Formula. The Three Section Formula involves beginning your cadenza with the theme from the concerto that will transition into a development section with sequences, altered themes, more virtuosic runs, and passages in thirds. This all leads to the final part of the cadenza, where the soloist will end with a trill leading the orchestra back in.

Write down the different sections of your cadenza on a piece of paper, like this:

- Statement of theme (with a transition to development)
- Develop the theme
- Ending and final trill

As you look at "Statement of Theme" on the piece of paper, play from memory the theme or themes of your concerto. Then as you look at the label "Transition to Development," improvise a transition to the development section, so on and so forth. The development section can include sequences, altered thematic material, fast diatonic runs, passages in thirds, and arpeggiated lines based on diminished chords. As for harmony, think about altering the tonality to closely related keys when you are in the development section (just try not to veer too far from the central tonality). As the development section ends, make sure to return to the original tonal center. I would encourage you to explore harmony by creating successive chords that create tension and then resolve the tension. Try these chord progressions:

1. I ii V I
2. I IV V I
3. I64 V

Practice by first learning each chord in each progression by outlining the arpeggio or stepwise motion . . . or both. Then, keeping these chords in mind, explore sequences, altered themes, virtuosic runs, and passages in thirds.

**Variations Exercise**

Improvise variations on a theme. First, improvise a simple melody—something like "Twinkle Twinkle Little Star." Then take the melody and subject it to different types of manipulation such as rhythmic alterations, change the major key to a minor key, a melodic variation with running embellishments, and harmonic variations.

Melodic Variation: Decorate and expand the melody. At first, try to make sure that the main melodic notes still land on the same beat as the original theme.

Rhythmic Variation: Alter the rhythm by breaking up the steady pulse and create syncopated off beats.

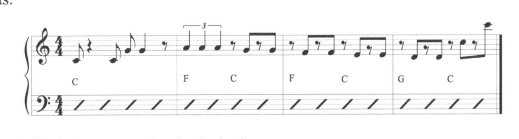

Harmonic Variation: create chord substitutions.

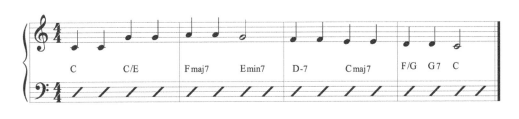

Major to Minor Mode

**Prologue Music Exercise**

1. Choose a piece of composed music that will follow the prologue music you will improvise.
2. Choose a key that relates to your chosen composed piece.
3. Choose a meter that relates to your chosen composed piece.
4. Choose a rhythmic or melodic motive from your chosen composed piece.
5. Improvise an eight-measure introduction that establishes the key. On the eighth bar, make sure to end on the dominant.
6. Using the chosen rhythmic or melodic motive as a model, play twelve bars of sequences or variations that relate closely to the tonic. On the eleventh bar, make sure to play the dominant of the home key, and on the twelfth bar, cadence on the tonic.

**Chance Music Exercises**

*One Musician Version:* Begin by choosing any series of pitches and rhythms by random methods such as rolling dice. For example: Assign a number to each of the 12 chromatic pitches in a typical Western chromatic scale. Roll dice four times to determine the four notes you will play (or whatever number of notes you want to use).

If the same number rolls out—if the same number rolls multiple times, you must use the note, even if that means you play the piece with only one note. Since it is impossible to roll a one with two dice, only use one die to find that last note on your final roll. Once you have the pitches for your improvised piece, begin to invent rhythmic patterns. Roll the dice one more time to determine how long each rhythmic pattern lasts—rolling a four could mean the rhythmic pattern lasts for four measures, etc.

*Multiple Musician Version:* Begin by choosing any series of pitches and rhythms by random methods such as rolling dice. For example: Assign a number to each of the 12 chromatic pitches in a typical Western chromatic scale. Roll dice four times to determine the four notes you will play (or whatever number of notes you want to use). If you roll the same number—if the same number rolls multiple times, you must use the note, even if that means you play the piece with only one note. Since it is impossible to roll a one with two dice, only use one die to find that last note on your final roll. Once you have the pitches for your improvised piece, begin to invent rhythmic patterns. Roll the dice one more time to determine how long each rhythmic pattern lasts—rolling a four could mean the rhythmic pattern lasts for four measures, etc. Then determine the order of entry for each musician. The piece ends when all players get through all of the notes and rhythmic patterns.

## Free Improvisation Exercise

This type of music focuses on timbre, rhythm, and melodic intervals and less about harmony. While the main elements of music (melody, harmony, and rhythm) are present, emphasis is placed more on mood, texture, and musicians' spontaneous interaction. This exercise is done best in a group setting. Begin by having one musician focus on timbre, rhythm, or set of melodic intervals. At this point, allow the rest of the ensemble to interact with one another, and create in the moment freely. Who comes in when, how long someone plays something, what someone plays, how things end, etc. are all determined in the moment of the spontaneous interaction of improvising musicians.

### *Essential Elements Applied to Classical Improvisation*

### 1. Trust

When I improvise, I *trust* my feelings. I trust that others in the ensemble will comprehend the moment when my solo will end. Conversely, others will trust me to be very clear about ending the solo. Trusting improvisers know how to end a piece of music through body language or hearing how the harmony leads to a conclusion.

### 2. Ability to Listen

I *listen* while I improvise as if it were a conversation. If I am truly listening, I am fully in the moment—not getting too excited about the next musical idea. Listening involves setting up the other ensemble members for success, creating musical lines to listen and react to easily. Listen to the point of being able to remember musical lines created earlier in the piece so that they can replicate or vary the idea later on in the piece.

### 3. Synergy

Chamber musicians who improvise work together to *synergize* their own ideas, helping to create the piece's structure. Anytime I have ever been a part of a chamber ensemble, classical or jazz, I make sure not to make the piece about me. Instead, I value placing the importance of the musical story over propelling my own individual arch. Letting go of one's own ideas when the idea does not fit with what the group is trying to achieve will help create a better synergistic group mindset.

### 4. Micromanagement and Macromanagement

When an improviser applies improvisation skills to early Western European music, it is important to think as a soloist and a composer. In the early days of the development of instrumental music, there was a reasonable expectation from composers that performers would improvise their music. So, when you improvise, think about how your embellishments or added material will help shape not only the melody but the entire piece as a whole.

### 5. Realization

My first jazz instructor, Earl Carter, once told me that improvisation is similar to archeology. The dinosaur fossils are there under the dirt, and it is the archeologist's job to unearth and discover

142    *Improvisation Exercises Inspired by Classical Genres*

them. The fossils, or in our case, the chord changes, are just dirt. Mr. Carter told me in a lesson once, "You must dig to unearth what the piece is about and discover how you can contribute to that conversation in a meaningful way." He taught me that once I am able to understand the conversation being had, I need to realize in the moment that the choices I make will either increase the value of that conversation and make it more interesting or drag it down. Understand the importance of being aware and knowing what needs to happen next in a piece. Realize the significance of balancing when to lead the musical line and when to support it—leaving room for others to create—and ultimately generating a better, more potent musical product. And most importantly, Mr. Carter helped me realize that "you must be patient and only enter when you can add value to the chart."

## 6. Stepping into the Deep

Do not be afraid to try something new and different—especially when you are first learning how to improvise. As hard as it might be, try your best not to feel like you've made a colossal mistake. Mistakes are part of the learning process. When students of mine make a mistake, I tell them to allow the mistake to refine them and not define them. *Refine* meaning to keep playing, performing, and learning from the mistakes, allowing the mistake to make them stronger and better equipped for the next opportunity.

## 7. Confidence

In the chapter three anecdote, Mary was the last performer to enter into the improvised piece. As a flute player, she could have created a number of interesting musical elements. She had the *confidence* in understanding the role her instrument had in that particular moment. She knew that starting low and then, as the phrase ended, growing louder and higher would add to the piece's value. She also had the confidence not to play until the climax of larger sections. The idea came from the nature of the piccolo itself. If she played too soon, she would probably have dominated the piece, and since the group sounded well put together, she did not want to dominate, rather just add color and flare. Having confidence in grasping the nature of one's instrument will aid in creating higher-level artistic real-time compositions.

## 8. Genuine Study of Craft

Remember that these exercises are a tool to help apply the intention to invention process to an applied style. Take these exercises as a springboard to the next step—an in-depth study of treatises and stylistic nuance based on time period and region.

## 9. Practice

No matter how much time someone spends listening, analyzing, or studying historical documents, there is no substitution for the time spent in the practice room. Practicing is more than just learning the notes or applying the concepts. It is about the ability to transform from a musician developing the coordination of the technique to one who uses the instrument as an extension of themselves. Whether the application of improvisation is Baroque music, jazz music, or any kind of music, players must make sure that the technical challenges are taken care of in the practice room to allow them to focus on the creation of music and not just the processing of notes.

# 10. Imagination

Imagine for a moment what it was like living in Europe before 1850. Imagine yourself as a court musician. When you get past a basic understanding of "the rules" and the technical challenges of your instrument, then it is important to bring your improvisation to life. Do the research and discover what the piece is about, why the composer wrote it, who commissioned it, etc. This discovery will help awaken your imagination. If the piece was for a dance, then as you play the piece, imagine someone dancing while you play.

Here is a fun exercise that can help awaken the imagination. The Silent Film Exercise is a fun exercise inspired by the musicians, typically organists/keyboard players, who improvised the soundtrack during screenings of silent movies during the early stages of film. There are three levels of the Silent Film Exercise—cartoon, TV, movie. In each level of exercise, the musicians must play music that matches the mood, style, and pacing of the visual they accompany without prior viewing. Not only does this develop improvisational skills, but it also requires a wide variety of different types of applications such as jazz and classical, as well as developing stamina to play for a significant amount of time.

## Multiple Genre Exercises: Silent Film

### Level 1: Cartoon

Watch an episode from a cartoon series, such as *Looney Tunes*, *Tom and Jerry*, or *The Simpsons*, etc., with the sound completely turned off, subtitles turned on, and improvise the score to it. In this exercise, focus your attention to the action. For example, in *Tom and Jerry*, there is a lot of action that occurs throughout. Watch the action and react musically to what you see. At this point, do not worry about character development, musical motifs, developing melody, etc. Just watch and react musically. This exercise can be done by oneself or with others.

### Level 2: Television

Watch the first episode from a television series, such as *Breaking Bad*, *Homeland*, *Game of Thrones*, etc., with the sound turned off, subtitles turned on, and improvise the score to it. The goal is to improvise the score to one episode. In this exercise, focus your attention on creating motifs for the main characters. Then alter the melodies in relationship and support of the character in the different situations of next week's episode. Think about the main melodies and their relationships to character development and how you would develop the melody accordingly. I recommend starting with episode one and working your way through until the season/series finale. This exercise can be done by oneself or with others.

### Level 3: Movies

As the title suggests, pick a full-length feature film of any genre. Turn off the sound, and turn on the subtitles. In this exercise, you are improvising the score to the film as you watch it in real time. The goal is to adequately represent the action sequences, the character development, etc. through musical methods. One of the biggest challenges is to stay focused and engaged in the creative process for the typical 120-minute movie length. In this exercise, there is much more long-term real-time musical thinking. Create and develop melodies like you did in the

144 *Improvisation Exercises Inspired by Classical Genres*

TV exercise, but as the plot thickens and the character develops over the entire movie, so should your melodies. Additionally, more action sequences appear in movies, as well as dialogue, so make sure to support musically everything that you see. This exercise can be done by oneself or with others.

The ability to stay focused for a significant amount of time, involving multiple genres of music, reacting instantly to the visual, is something silent movie musicians did all the time. But what if it wasn't a movie? What if an improvising musician had to maintain focus for a significant amount of time, needed multiple music genres, and instantly reacted to the visual? Oh, but wait! What if the visual was also improvised? What if the musician also had to compose full-length songs and other supportive material but never saw it before because the live actors improvised everything?

# 12 Understanding Improv Comedy Language

Wyatt, the theater's artistic director, asked the summer music director, "Joe, we have an improv comedy troupe associated with the theater. You want in?"

Joe replied, "Oh, I've seen something like that on TV."

Wyatt continued, "No, it's not like what you've seen on TV, it's long-form improv comedy."

"What's long-form improv comedy?" Joe asked.

Wyatt explained, "Long-form improv comedy is the purest form of improvised storytelling. Compared to short form, it has less structure, relying less on gimmicks and audience input without any prescribed games, which gives the players more creative freedom but also more room to fail."

Joe, in a sarcastic tone, said, "No structure with more room to fail, completely improvised in front of an audience? Sounds stressful. Where do I sign up?"

## Long-Form Improv Comedy—What It Is and How It Incorporates Live Music

Long form improvisational comedy can be *stressful*; however, it is really a matter of one's mindset and can be more of an adrenaline rush rather than a stressful event. In my circumstance, Wyatt wanted music to be a part of his improv troupe. In this case, long form takes shape as a variety of scenes, with some including music. It is up to me, the musical improviser, to decide when music happens. For example, if there is a scene where there is a lot of talking with no music, perhaps the next scene is where two people are trying to give directions to one another, and the musical improviser inserts a song. Long form has more room for character development and storytelling since it does not need to abide by a specific game to drive the scene. Situation, character, and story together drive the scene in long form. Long-form improvisational comedy with an added musical element can be a scary experience for the novice. The novice may be scared that she will somehow make a mistake and mess up the scene. She needs to remember that as an improviser, she must listen to her surroundings. In order to help propel the situation, character, or story, she must be an active listener just as much as a dynamic performer. Therefore, the musical improviser begins to incorporate music into this style of improvisation by exhibiting intense high levels of listening and then reacting to what the actors are projecting. Specifically, she should focus on the actors' story and then attempt to play something that she thinks might work and fit in with the scene.

## Do We Need Musical Accompaniment in This Form? If So, What For?

While my troupe wanted music to be a part of their comedy team, do all troupes have music? Is there a need for music? The answer is no. There is no need for musical accompaniment in

DOI:10.4324/9781003341857-12

long-form improvisational comedy. A scene in this form, if done well, can be perfectly executed with its own pace, rhythm, and texture without the need for musical accompaniment. However, musical accompaniment greatly enhances the improv comedy style because it adds another layer to the improvisation experience. Since this is long-form improv, where the situation, character, and storytelling drive the scene, music is an important element, just as it is significant in other storytelling idioms such as movies and live theater. Audiences have such a visceral response to music. Music can emphasize an underlying psychology, drawing out certain emotions. It can also heighten tension or stakes or joy, etc. in the moment. The added music can trigger a reaction in an audience that no other form of improvisation can accomplish. If done well, musical accompaniment helps give the show variety, raises the stakes of a scene, and sometimes can save the scene. In addition, an actor attempting to perform an unwritten song can generate an added layer of humor for the audience.

As an actor began to create a scene, I accidentally hit two notes on the keyboard. The actor reacted physically to the notes. I was shocked and didn't think the actor would respond to my mistake. I thought I was just someone there to provide underscore, sound effects, or potentially a song but not an equal member. However, this time, I was the other "actor" in the scene. Without saying anything, the improv actor and I created a scene in which he played a man who got frustrated with trying to fix his doorbell; it would never sound precisely when he wanted it to sound. The scene continued, escalating to more and more frustration until the very end, where I played the doorbell exactly when the actor wanted it.

## What Is a Musical Improviser?

The light bulb (or rather doorbell) moment for me was when I changed my mindset from being a musical accompanist to considering myself an equal player in the troupe, just with a different voice. While the role of a musical improviser is to create sound effects, underscore scenes, or create songs for the actors to sing on the spot, your mindset in this setting must be the same as an actor's mindset—following the same rules an improv actor would follow. Hence, a musical improviser is an actor who uses a piano (or any other instrument) as his main voice to participate in the improvised scene, helping propel the scene along or add new information. If not, then stay out of the way. A musical improviser is a third-person entry. A third-person entry at the basic level is when a third actor joins a two-person scene. The musical improviser has the choice of being either a third person entry or a third wheel. He can either add to a scene or create awkwardness in a scene. Choose to add to a scene.

## What Makes a Third Wheel Entry?

- The third wheel enters and derails the scene.
- The third wheel pulls focus away from the events or relationships of the scene.
- The third wheel values a silly gag over the content of the scene.
- The third wheel is confusing and not clear.
- The third wheel does not add to good storytelling.
- The third wheel makes it about him or her.

## What Makes a Good Third-Person Musical Improviser Entry?

- The third person creates an engaging environment or atmosphere.
- The third person is aware when a scene has not found its legs and helps by entering into the scene to move it forward.
- The third person understands where the scene is going and, if need be, does not enter.

There are three main types of helpful third person entries.

### 1. Add to the Environment

a. Improv Comic Actor Example: An actor enters as a waiter in a restaurant where two people are on a date. The waiter makes a conscious decision not to make the scene about him or her, rather building the atmosphere around the other two people.

b. Musical Improviser Example: The scene involves two people on a date in a fancy restaurant. Fancy restaurants have live music. This music typically is solo classical piano, violin, or guitar. So the musical improviser starts playing very soft classical music in the background to create an atmosphere of elegant dining.

### 2. Here Comes Charlie

a. Improv Comic Actor Example: Similar to the short-form improv game, where two people in a scene talk about a third person who is not in the scene. They then make it clear that this person needs to enter at some point. They are building their world and setting up others to come in as those characters.

b. Musical Improviser Example: The scene is about a mother and daughter at the beach trying to have an intimate conversation, but they keep talking about the odd number of birds flying around them. As the musical improviser, this is a signal to start adding sound effects. The actors are talking about birds, so it would be appropriate to add different bird sounds to help legitimize their description or raise the stakes by eventually adding dog and cat sound effects.

### 3. Raising the Stakes

a. Improv Comic Actor Example: The actors are trying to find the scene, but they are not able to discover it or perhaps unable to find a closing capper line. An actor in the wings has a brilliant idea on what to add and decides, for example, that

    i. she is a singing telegram who comes to the door and sings about how the main character's wife leaves him, thus inventing a purpose to the scene and its characters;

    ii. she suddenly joins a scene as a television reporter who declares a mad man is on the loose, thus creating another layer and a focal point for the scene;

    iii. in a deeply emotional scene between two people with seemingly no end in sight, he or she comes out as a Starbucks barista and says, "Are you guys ready to order yet?" thus creating a funny moment due to the emotional scene happening in front of the Starbucks barista;

b. Musical Improviser Example: The musical improviser can insert a made-up song in any of the previous scenes. A third-person entry breaks down to this: Am I making the scene more interesting, or am I just adding something to add something? The goal is for the entry to raise the stakes or clarify information, helping the main characters tell the story better, frame them in some way that creates a more interesting setting for where they are in the scene, or reinforces the fears or dreams of one particular character. For a musical improviser, an exciting and challenging way to do this is by making up songs.

## How a Musical Improviser Makes Up a Song

Musical improvisers need to have the ability to recognize the moment when a song should or could happen to raise the stakes or help propel a scene forward. A musical improviser needs confidence and a willingness to jump in headfirst without hesitation. She must focus on what is happening to jump in at the right moment and give the other actors the gift of a song to help propel the story or make something funny or whatever. The musical improviser must be "on the same page" as the other actors. She must have a high level of focused listening and anticipation of what might come next, where she can find that "click moment"—the moment when everyone knows that the only thing that has to happen is a song. Musical improvisers are patient and will wait for the right moment. The actors have to trust that the musical improviser will come in at the exact right moment.

### *How Does One Know When to Come in to Do Those Things Such as Raising the Stakes, Etc.?*

It happens very quickly. One must be in storyteller mindset, looking for ways to raise the stakes or define the environment. Listen to the scene; understand what they are talking about and where it might lead. Then, just like in a musical, where would it make sense to add a song? Are they in love and one of the characters is about to ask the other to marry him? Perhaps the answer could be in song form. Or a husband and a wife are arguing, and the wife asks the husband, "Why don't you ever take out the trash?" The husband could sing the reply as to why he didn't take out the trash, and the "game" of the scene then becomes each question the wife asks her husband, he answers in song. Then perhaps by the end, they both work out their issues through song. The musical improviser will know the perfect moment to enter if one is in a heightened listening state and storyteller mindset. Thus, the musical improviser must listen and trust himself enough not to hesitate and miss the moment, or even worse: hesitate, miss the moment, and then come in anyway.

There is no ounce of being timid when a musical improviser comes into a scene with a song. She is decisive, knows when to come into the scene, and will make the scene better. And when the musical improviser ends songs, she is again very decisive. Actors need a musician who is confident and can lead the formal structure of the song when they are improvising lyrics. Musical improvisers also go along with the scene musically or purposely juxtapose the scene. For example, if the scene involves two people in love, the song will be a ballad to express their love for one another. Or perhaps instead of a love song, the musical improviser decides to play a disco song for the two to dance out their feelings for one another.

The most successful musical improvisers in this style have experience with multiple genres, musical theater, and composition. They are comfortable with improvising within a simple song form and have knowledge and experience of the dramatic structure of musical theater. Musical improvisers must synthesize their skills as musicians and apply them to acting in a scene.

## The Construction of an Improv Comedic Song

Pay special attention to the harmonic progression. The harmonic progression needs to be simple enough for the improvising singer to internalize the notes, clearing up his or her mind to focus on what lyrics to make up.

Some of the most popular songs are popular because they a number of common tone chords and are repetitive. Sticking to a simple I-IV-V-I chord progression is a good start for improvising songs. The more experience not only with making up songs but making up songs with the same people, the more harmonically interesting a song can be—modulating, tritone subs, adding ii-V, chromatic mediants, etc.

The easiest way to spontaneously create the correct style is for the musical improviser to focus on the scene's action and wait intensely. As she does, she discovers the scene right alongside the actors on stage. This discovery will lead the musical improviser to play a style of music that best represents the objective of the scene.

# 13 Improvisation for the Improv Comedic Musician

**How an Improv Comic Actor Makes Up Lyrics to a Song**

How does a comedic actor improvise songs? The actor needs to understand that the piano player is just as much a scene partner as another actor, and the piano player needs to think like an actor. The comedic actor needs to ask herself: *What does my scene partner (the pianist) see in what I just did in the scene that necessitated her to add a song in that exact moment?* The comedic actor also needs to ask herself: *What is the most important thing that my character needs to say now and what sort of emotional journey does my character need to go on at this point? Can I propel the story forward within the song itself, or is this just about how I feel in the moment?*

Two critical elements actors should focus on are (1) identifying the most significant aspect to their character and (2) discovering what they are trying to do to the other character in the scene—but in song form. Another part of the actor's mindset is to listen to the sequence of chords to get a sense of the harmonic progression. This is an important factor to focus on, especially when the actor tries to find the right note to sing. In addition, the actor is adjusting to the style of music presented by the musical improviser in order to match that style vocally. Finally, the singer needs to create a chorus or hook that other ensemble members can sing along. All of this happens in an introduction of about ten to fifteen seconds.

**Improvising Lyrics**

Wyatt understood that for his audience, one of the most impressive things to watch as an audience is when an improv comic has to improvise a song. My main role is to create underscore, sound effects, and songs for the actors to make up lyrics, essentially third-person entries. The underscore would represent whatever scene takes place in the moment. For example, if it were a scary scene, I would play scary music. Sound effects were more or less easy for me to anticipate—if the scene opened with two actors playing baseball, I would have at the ready a swinging of a bat sound, a bat hitting a ball sound, and crowds cheering sound. The songs were a bit more challenging. While my background in jazz led me to create simple I-IV-V-I chord progressions that were easy for actors to sing to, making up lyrics was still hard for some actors. So I asked myself, How can I help actors make up lyrics on the spot?

The improv singer must understand the difference between the two main parts of a song—a verse and a chorus. While the song's form can vary, typically after the introduction, the verse is sung twice (verse 1 and verse 2), and the chorus follows. After the chorus, one could go back and sing two more verses and then repeat the chorus one final time to end the song.

DOI:10.4324/9781003341857-13

I think of verses as being more narrative, musically subtle, more conversational, more rhythmic, and less melodic than a chorus. They have more words that inform the audience rather than expressing a feeling. Verses have shorter note values and are not as melodic as a chorus. The harmonic structure is open and will always drive to the chorus. The purpose of the verse should set the premise that describes the subject. When the verse repeats, the words should change. Harmonically, the characteristic of a verse when improvising a song should involve minimal chords, with little rhythmic drive to allow the actor to focus on getting the verse information expressed. Then when the chorus happens, the harmony can involve more common tone chords that allow the actor to elongate the vowel and convey a feeling.

Characteristics of a *chorus* involve fewer words that are lyrical with more extended value notes. It is the most expressive reaction to the information provided in the verse. It states the main point or message of the song with less rhythmic motion and more melodic contour. Since the harmonic structure of a chorus is closed, lyric repetition is acceptable and encouraged when singing the second chorus. The subject of the chorus can be the key motivating desire in an "I Want" type song, or the point of view such as in an "Act I Finale" type song, a reason why the bad guy is hated in a "Villain" type song, or perhaps what was learned in a "Finale" type song.

There are numerous approaches in which a song can take form. What follows is an outline of the most common types of verse/chorus connections a song may possess. Whatever the scene's subject may be, if the musical improviser sees her moment and adds a song, the improvising singer will know which connection to use.

## 1. What/Feel
In the what/feel connection, the purpose of the verse is to describe the subject in very specific ways. The lyrics do not need to rhyme; they just need to make sense in explaining the qualities of the subject. Then in the chorus, the singer should express how they feel about the subject. For example:

*Verse 1:* Describe the subject that you are singing: "Dragons are green, dragons are neat, I'd like a green one, and I'd call him Pete."

*Verse 2:* Describe the subject that you are singing, but use different lyrics: "Flying all day on his winged back, enjoying the view of our fire-spewing attack."

*Chorus:* After describing the subject, express how it makes you feel: "Being with dragons makes me feel so great, it's better than the Garden or the Sunshine State."

## 2. What/How
In the what/how connection, the purpose of the verse is to describe the subject, typically a place one wants to go. It is similar to the "what/feel" connection, but in the chorus, the singer expresses how they will get to the place they are describing. For example:

*Verse:* Describe the place you want to go: "I want to be where the people are, a bustling place filled with daytime work and nightlife adventure. Where . . . in a city never sleeping . . ."

*Verse 2:* Describe the place you want to go, but use different lyrics: "I want to live in the concrete jungle, swinging from tall buildings and breathing smog."

*Chorus:* After describing the subject, express how you will get there: "I will get there, I will find a way. I will take a train or British Airways."

## 3. Opposites

In the opposites connection, the purpose of the verse is to describe elements contrary to the central subject outlined in the chorus. In the chorus, express the definition of the central subject. A great example is the Beach Boys song "California Girls":

*Verse:* "East Coast girls are . . . and Midwest girls are . . ." The singer is describing all the things California Girls (the subject) are not.

*Chorus:* Then when the singer arrives at the chorus, he sings, "But I wish they all could be California girls."

## 4. Question/Answer

In the question/answer connection, the purpose of the verse is to ask yourself questions, such as *Am I good enough? Can I do this? Will I succeed? Do I really want it? Do I deserve it?* It's essentially questioning yourself. The purpose of the chorus is to answer the questions. For example:

*Verse:* "Do I really want this? Am I ready? Do I have the strength to go on? There is no end in sight, I cannot see the light. I'm not sure if this is right."

*Verse 2:* "Do I dare or do I not? Can I do it? Am I the right man for the job? They say I'm not that good. Or just misunderstood. Not sure if I should or could."

*Chorus:* You answer the questions with "Yes, I can do it, I will succeed. Yes, I can do it, I believe."

## 5. Lead to Why

In the lead to why connection, the verse is a backstory. The backstory will lead to the chorus that expresses why, for example, you hate cheese.

*Verse 1:* "Many years ago, when I was a kid, my dad worked for a dairy farm outside of Madrid. It snowed a lot and it was cold, with many cows, and lots of mold."

*Verse 2:* "There was a time once when I loved my cheese. But then my older brother made me eat the green fuzz, and it made me wheeze."

*Chorus:* "I hate cheese. There's nothing gouda bout it."

## 6. The Conversation

In the conversation, there may or may not be a chorus. The main purpose of this type of song is to have a conversation set to music. This is similar to the recitative style in opera. The two actors rhythmically match the form of the chord progression, speak-singing the words they would use in conversation.

*Verse:* Character 1—"I told you not to leave. I told you not to go. Listen to me now or you'll end up on skid row."

*Verse:* Character 2—"I am eighteen now and can do what I desire. I can vote, smoke, buy a boat, or even start a fire."

*Verse:* Character 1—"Don't be stupid, don't be dumb, don't be naive. You have no job or money or a college degree."

*Verse:* Character 2—"I'll do what I want. I'll do what I wish. There's no stopping me now." Character 1: "You're being foolish."

## 7. Point of View

The point of view type song is challenging. This song involves multiple characters who have different points of view that work advantageously toward a common goal. This is an advanced level of improvised singing for a group of improvisers with high levels of group-mindedness. In point of view, there are a series of verses, with each character having their own verse/point of view. After the verses, there is a chorus that combines all of the verses all at once. After the first chorus performance, a hook is discovered, and all the members sing the refrain. For example:

*Verse 1:* Protagonist—"I feel scared but I will fight on"—the fate of the journey

*Verse 2:* Protagonist Sidekick—"I will help you, don't give up"—encouragement

*Verse 3:* Loved One/Victim—"Save me, help me, you will find me"—help me

*Verse 4:* Villain—"My plan will succeed"—the opposite of the protagonist

*Verse 5:* Sidekick—"You will win"—supports the villain

*Chorus 1:* A combination of all five together.

*Chorus 2:* One person (typically the protagonist) finds a hook. The hook in this type of song could be about the subject of the scene. If the subject is finding love, then use one of the aforementioned song types to create a hook based on the subject of love.

## Improvising Lyrics

### *Strategies to Improvise Songs*

If an improv actor can improvise lines in a scene, then an improv actor can improvise lyrics in a song. The only difference is setting it inside a particular musical framework and being able to create the poem of the lyrics within the time as quickly as it takes for the introduction to be performed.

### *Exercise 1: Creating Lyrics in the Moment*

1. **Focus on the want.** This is the point of your song. It is what you are trying to communicate. For example: wanting to be a pilot.

2. **Word association.** The next step is to create word associations with the want. The want of becoming a pilot can be associated with the words *fly, high, sky, plane, far away, jet, birds, airlines,* and *wings.*

3. **Describe it.** Imagine what it is like to be a pilot. Describe what they look like, what it takes to be a pilot, or perhaps what it is that they actually do: "Pilots are cool, they're really smart, they fly really high in the sky."

4. **Form a verse.** Focusing on the want, thinking of words associated with the want, and describing the want, the actor can form these words into a verse: "Wouldn't it be great to . . . imagine flying?"

   a. Make sure to break the verse into phrases. Typically, this is a two- or four-bar phrase.
   b. Be narrative, but don't ramble.
   c. Have a beginning and end to your thought.
   d. Keep things short and simple.

5. **Form a chorus.** The verse/chorus connection that you choose will dictate how you shape the chorus. Regardless of which connection is chosen, the singing improviser should focus in the moment on finding one or two words that best express the relationship to the information provided in the verse and elongate the vowels of those chosen words. For example, should the improviser choose *fly*, *high*, and *sky* as their main words, the shape of the chorus will be longer-valued notes and elongated vowels.

6. **Finding your note.** For improv actors who do not possess a high level of music theory or vocal training, attempting to find the right note may be a challenge. There are two solutions to this problem. The first is that it is ok not to sound like a trained vocalist in this style. In many ways, it is funnier when the improv singer does not sound good but kills it with the lyrics and comedic energy. The second answer is to pick any note that fits in with what the pianist is playing. Trust your ear to dictate what is pleasing and what is unpleasing. If the pianist plays a chord progression that involves common tone chords, then the improvising singer will have an easier time finding other notes to sing, since common tone chords share some of the same notes that will work when the chord changes. Suppose, for some reason, they still cannot find the note. In that case, I suggest that the improvised singer sing a note either a little higher or a little lower than the note he is on, stays on the note, and hopefully when the chord changes the note will fit or the pianist will alter the chord to fit the note you are singing.

*Exercise 2: Developing Improvisation for the Individual and Collective Mind*

1. In order to develop both an individual and group mind collective improvised song, try utilizing the Point of View verse/chorus connection. For the Point of View song, the improvising singer needs to identify his or her point of view and comprehend how to construct the singing of that point of view musically. As an exercise, try this:

### *Creating an individual group mind—Verse*

a. Label five improv actor/singers as a protagonist, a protagonist's sidekick, a loved one or victim of circumstance, an antagonist, and an antagonist's sidekick. As the collective advances, increase the number of different characters.
b. Have the accompanist create a harmonic progression conducive to singers improvising a verse, for example, a simple I-IV-V-I progression. As the collective improves, have the accompanist create a new accompaniment verse for each character.
c. First entrance is the protagonist: Sing the point of view like a verse, offering information of whatever the protagonist is working to accomplish.
d. Second entrance is the protagonist's sidekick: Sing this point of view lyrically like a chorus with long value notes, elongating vowels without a large number of words.
e. Third entrance is the loved one/victim: Sing this point of view lyrically like a chorus; however, musically make it more of a supporting role, perhaps in counterpoint to the protagonist's friend. If he goes high, the loved one/victim should go low.
f. Fourth entrance is the antagonist: Similar to the protagonist, sing this point of view like a verse, offering information of whatever the protagonist is working to accomplish; however,

the note choices and rhythmic choices should be in counterpoint with the protagonist. If the protagonist finishes a phrase, the antagonist should begin hers. If there is a certain rhythm that the protagonist has created, mimic this rhythm.

g. Fifth entrance is the antagonist's sidekick: Similar to the protagonist's friend, sing this point of view lyrically like a chorus with long-value notes, elongating vowels without a large number of words and supporting whatever the villain is creating.

### *Creating an individual group mind—Chorus*

a. After the fifth character has sung his verse, all characters sing what they sang in their own verse but all together at the same time. After the first statement of this section, the next chorus, led by the protagonist, creates a hook for the loved one and the protagonist's sidekick to sing. After this statement of the chorus, the last chorus repeats with the antagonist and the antagonist sidekick adding a countermelody.

*Exercise 3: Call for the Song*

In this exercise, every scene created will have a song. Ideally, the exercise should allow for whatever type of verse/chorus connection makes sense with whatever is created in the scene; nonetheless, it is important to make sure all connections are developed in order to be ready for the moment should it happen in performance, so make sure to practice all connections.

1. Call for the song: **What/Feel**
   A typical scene involving a what/feel connection could resemble Samwise Gamgee asking Frodo Baggins what is so special about the world beyond the shire.

2. Call for the song: **What/How**
   A typical scene involving a what/how connection could resemble a daughter being told she can't be an astronaut by an authority figure. At the same time, she still secretly dreams of being an astronaut.

3. Call for the song: **Opposites**
   A typical scene involving an opposites connection could be something resembling a 25-year-old first-year lawyer trying to buy his first new car. He is offered many different makes and models of cars, but his favorite car is the Chevy Cavalier, and nothing is better than a Chevy Cavalier.

4. Call for the song: **Question/Answer**
   A typical scene involving a question/answer connection could resemble a young man about to ask his girlfriend of two years to marry him. Right before he asks, he questions himself as to whether it will go well and explores his doubts.

5. Call for the song: **Lead to Why**
   While the lead to why is typically a backstory, the lead to why could also be associated with a scene resembling a mom talking to her kids about the importance of picking up their toys.

6. Call for the song: **The Conversation**
   A typical scene involving a conversation connection could resemble a married couple arguing about who's responsible for taking out the trash.

## 156 *Improvisation for the Improv Comedic Musician*

7. Call for the song: **Point of View**

   Calling for a song involving a point-of-view connection can get tricky. There are a lot of people on stage for this. I recommended that the actors predetermine each person's role and point of view to utilize this exercise successfully. The point of view connection can be used in any number of group ensemble scenes; for example, the group scene could be a situation wherein they all learn something important. Each person sings about what they have learned in the verses, and everyone sings the one thing that connects them all in the chorus.

### *Essential Elements for the Improv Comedic Musician*

### 1. Trust

Successful improv comic actors/singers and musical improvisers exhibit high levels of trust with one another. The improv actor/singer trusts that the musical improviser will create a song that makes sense within the scene and place the song in the exact moment it needs to happen. The musical improviser needs to trust that the scene will play out the way it plays out, and if a song is not needed, then he should not create a song. The singer must trust that she will know in the moment which verse/chorus connection to make. Utilizing the exercises will have instilled in her the ability to create lyrics. Success in this style of improvisation is trusting the process even though there may not be a product in sight.

### 2. Ability to Listen

Listen intently to the subject of the scene. I concentrate on the unique tone of each character, the relationship between the characters, and where the scene is progressing. I listen for how a type or mood of a song could match what is being created on stage and for the exact moment to have the song enter. If there is focused listening both by the musical improviser to the actors and by the actors to the musical improviser, then each group will feed the other what is needed.

### 3. Synergy

With many players involved, the musical improvisers and the comedic actors must have a synergistic approach to the goal. Recognize that when a musical improviser comes in with a song, he is essentially a third-person entry; however, once he enters, he provides the direction, giving all the gifts needed to improvise a song vocally. If the song is placed well, the singer will know the style, the verse/chorus connection, the point of the scene, etc.

### 4. Micromanagement and Macromanagement

If I happen to be working with other musicians, then in addition to what I am trying to create, my focus is also on what the other person is creating. It is critical in a performance setting to work in tandem with others to form a group mind connection, where all parties think simultaneously at the macro and micro levels. Here, macro refers to the goal of the piece of music, and micro refers to the players' grasp of where they are in the present and from the present how to achieve the larger musical goal. Group improvisation typically involves two or more musicians (or actors) engaging in a musical conversation. The conversation should not have one participant who constantly "talks" or interrupts the other. This creates an environment that is not much fun to participate in or listen to, and it does not produce a positive constructive result. Instead, it should be an equal exchange of ideas that develop naturally.

## 5. Realization

Realize that this style of improvisation relies heavily on a group mind collective. All group members, actors, and musical improvisers must understand and agree with what is being done or suggested. They must go along with the best idea while enhancing what they think will add to the momentum of that great idea. When the improvisation goes well, all players realize the same objective and how to achieve the goal.

## 6. Stepping into the Deep

Make sure not to fall into the same patterns. As the group mind develops, strive as a musical improviser to take bigger risks—if successful, the bigger the risk, the bigger the reward. Examples of risk-taking include calling back a scene with a song, juxtaposing a song style that audiences would not expect in the scene, or beginning a scene with music.

## 7. Confidence

The most important element of improvisation for a musical improviser to exude is confidence. Many variables are involved with songs in long-form improvisation; therefore, improvisers must create a constant that grounds the variables. The constant is the musical improviser's confidence that the song enters at the perfect moment where the actor/singer instantly knows the verse/chorus connection. The musician's harmony and structure are such that they give the actor/singer confidence that they will find their note and that it will be an efficaciously creative moment.

## 8. Genuine Study of Craft

At times during a performance, I have observed that my level of awareness in the moment was so high that I found it challenging to know what was happening outside of the focused intent. After years of extensive practice and performance experience, I believe a successful improviser exhibits intense levels of focused listening and reacts accordingly to the musical environment in the moment.

## 9. Practice

I found myself over the years thinking about how whenever I'm in an improv rehearsal, it really is not about me. The practice isn't about learning my part; it is about learning other people's roles. The more I learned about the other people in the ensemble, the better I anticipated their actions.

## 10. Imagination

I believe that imagination is a critical part of the improv process for this style of music. As the musical improviser, you must feel like an equal member of the improv troupe. You are present, in the moment, actively improvising the long-form improvised story along with the actors. Use your imagination, and think of ways you can help support the scene.

# 14 Liturgical Improvisation
## Traditional and Contemporary

Most of the music for liturgical services are written out and preplanned; however, there are times when improvising music is appropriate and, in some cases, required. Music that is not sufficient to cover, for example, a ritual activity, would need to be improvised until the action is over. Areas throughout the mass that can be improvised include hymn introductions, offertory, communion, and postludes. While improvising music can be utilitarian, as a church musician, it is important to improvise music so you can influence the congregation's experience.

Not everyone experiences music the same way; however, music is a language, and there is some commonality. For example, within a given society, we can all recognize a fanfare-like passage and relate a similar meaning to it. We know what scary music sounds like, that is some would say, diminished chords in a low register, or loud high screeching passages. Music that is fast can relate to excitement, and slower music can relate to sadness or reflection. Even though the congregation may not experience music in the same exact way every time they hear it, it is important for a church musician to inspire and communicate the feeling of the text. The first part of this chapter will examine the Catholic Mass and its need for improvised music. All of the skills in this chapter can be applied to other denominations. The second half of this chapter will discuss contemporary christian worship music.

**The Catholic Mass and Music: Outline of Roman Catholic Mass for Musicians**

Prelude—music that happens before the mass
Gathering Hymn—the opening hymn to gather everyone together to begin the mass
Kyrie—a prayer sung
Gloria—a prayer sung
Responsorial Psalm—a psalm from the Book of Psalms in the Old Testament (typically sung)
Gospel Acclamation—a congregation's greeting (typically sung) of the gospel
Offertory—the presentation and preparation of the gifts (bread and wine)
Sanctus—a prayer sung
Memorial Acclamation—a Eucharistic prayer (typically sung)
Amen—a culminating point of the eucharistic prayer section of the mass (typically sung)
Agnus Dei—a prayer sung
Communion—a meditative time where the congregation communes with God
Closing Hymn—a piece to celebrate the end of the mass
Postlude—an optional piece of music as people are leaving the church

## Season and Calendar

The liturgical year begins on the first Sunday of Advent (which is about four weeks before Christmas) and runs through to the last Sunday of the liturgical year called Christ the King—which typical occurs in late November. You might recognize the seasons that occur throughout an entire liturgical calendar which includes Advent, Christmas, Lent, Easter, and Ordinary Time.

There are three cycles of readings—Cycle A, Cycle B, and Cycle C. Each cycle has specific readings that are spoken during each week throughout the year. Over the course of three years (three yearly cycles), the majority of the Bible will have been read.

Music is determined by the readings—the readings have themes. The themes inform the music director to pick music to help support and propel the subject of a particular mass. There isn't a rule against playing an Easter or Christmas song out of season; however, most members of a congregation would think it odd.

Since the readings are determined by the yearly calendar, it is important for liturgical musicians to know what season they are in and which reading will be presented in order to adequately select the appropriate music for that particular service—it is about connecting the music to the readings and the season!

## Style of Improv Music

*Hymn Introductions:* Gathering hymns, or the opening hymn in a Mass, are similar to an overture of a musical. The hymn should be something the congregation knows and can sing. One of the purposes is to get the congregation energized and excited about the Mass. This is not the time to pick something obscure. The whole point of the opening hymn is to gather people together so they can pray as one. Recessionals, or the closing hymn, should be bigger and celebratory. Peter Latona, music director for the Basilica Shrine in Washington D.C., says,

I try to inspire the people to sing by communicating the feeling of the text. For example, in advent, an introduction could be something medieval sounding, with parallel fifths in a minor key, capturing the mysterious quality of the advent season, so when people sing the hymn, it has greater impact. In addition to hearing the pitch and tempo, a hymn introduction is an opportunity to reflect the character of the hymn.

*Offertory:* The offertory is where the bread and wine are prepared and ceremoniously placed on the altar. It occurs between the liturgy of the Word and the liturgy of the Eucharist. Think of the offertory as an intermission of sorts. Even though this part of the Mass can seem utilitarian, it is still important to communicate something. The music can be any number of styles, a larger choir piece, a hymn, an instrumental piece, etc. Should the need to improvise occur during the offertory, it is important to continue expressing the emotion until the action is complete. For example, if you program the hymn "Gift of Finest Wheat," you should strive to improvise music in the same vein and emotional direction as the lyrics suggest.

*Communion:* The communion part of the Mass is more laid-back. It is a meditative time, more pensive, more prayerful. The congregation just received the Eucharist and are praying. The music should characterize this pensive moment. To help develop your improvisation skills during this part of the Mass, I would 1) pay attention to the season of the liturgical calendar, study the readings for the week and discover the mood, 2) listen to the homily—was it uplifting, positive, thought-provoking? 3) think about what music was already sung earlier in the Mass to create a mood that relates to what was and then try to take the congregation deeper into prayer.

The key ingredient for improvisation in a liturgical setting is the use of the imagination to communicate something. Let the knowledge of the piece and the style of the moment ignite your imagination. Imagine sounds related to the information presented by the written material. Then use musical elements to support the imagination. How can one apply the intention to invention process to liturgical music? For many seasoned musicians, the answer to this question is "I've been doing it for a long time, so it's second nature." However, what happens if you haven't been doing this for a long time? Are there strategies in place to help a beginner improvise liturgical music?

## Liturgical Improvisation Strategies

### *Ostinato Options*

Ostinato is a figure or pattern that repeats. Practice using a variety of ostinato patterns. For example, try using triplet patterns, eighth note patterns, sixteenth note patterns to begin the learning process.

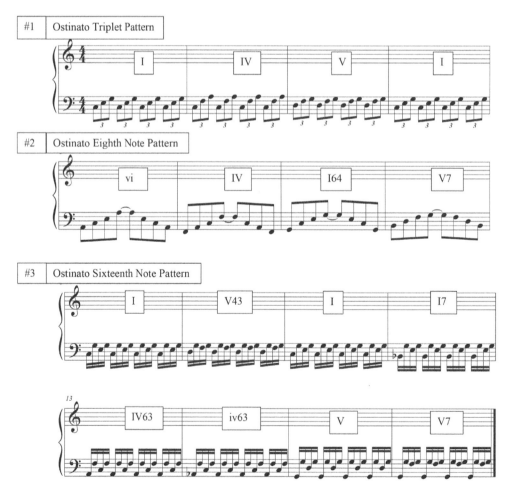

For example: Imagine that the prepared offertory music is complete, but you still need more music to cover the action near the alter, try this: Take the chord progression from the refrain of the selected offertory hymn (in this case, "Gift of Finest Wheat") and improvise by outlining the chords in the left hand and highlighting the chords in the right hand.

Then repeat the refrain by improvising an ostinato figure in the left hand.

### Harmonizing Options

Harmonizing a melody using fourths and fifths is a good starting point for some novice improvisers. To practice, try these options by harmonizing a major scale:

*Major scale with parallel fourths*

*Major scale with parallel fifths*

*Modify the rhythm*

*Arpeggiate in fourths*

*Stack fourths*

For example: Imagine that the prepared communion music is complete, but you still need more music to cover the action near the alter, try this: Take the chord progression from the refrain of the selected offertory hymn (in this case, "Here I Am Lord") and improvise by harmonizing the melody in the right hand and supporting simple chords in the left hand.

*Hymn Introduction Options*

Level One: Play the entire hymn once. See example: "Crown Him With Many Crowns." This is a good option if the hymn is short, or if the congregation is not familiar with the piece. A negative of this option is that there isn't any improvisation happening.

Level Two: Improvise a short flourish followed by the first four measures and then last four measures of the hymn. This is a good option if you are looking for an introduction that blends improvisation with some preplanning.

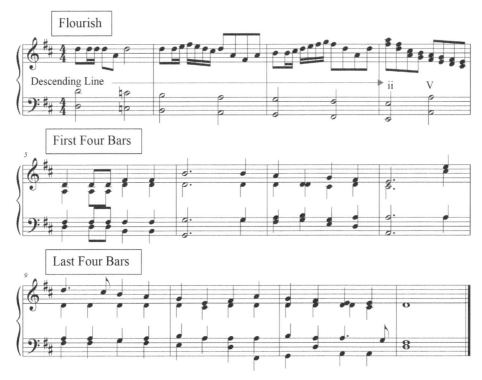

Level Three: improvise an extended introduction with elements of the hymn tune. This could be a good option because sometimes the size of the church makes it so that the processional takes a long time and thus necessitates a longer, more involved introduction. Or perhaps a congregation knows the hymn which can allow you to expand your musical choices. A negative could be that it may take time for the congregation to understand how the piece sounds, especially if they are not familiar with the hymn. Example of the last 16 bars of an extended 32 bar intro:

Begin with intro material like an ostinato, with supporting whole notes. Harmonically try using elements of the form of the hymn.

Then maintain the ostinato and harmonize elements of the melody

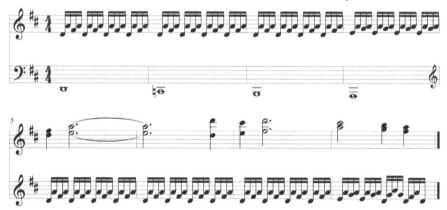

Then explore other key areas

Finally, play the last four bars of the hymn

## *Postlude Options*

Outline sketches of tunes for improvising a postlude.

Level One: Take a pre-composed melody and analyze the chord changes.
    Create a lead sheet.
Level Two: Improvise a melody and chord changes.

  In either level, create templates for yourself.

## For example:

Template 1:  In the right hand, you arpeggiate the harmony (with a woodwind texture if organ)
    In the left hand, there are simple chords played (with a string texture if organ)
    The main melody is played in the pedal (if organ)
Template 2:  In the right hand, play the main melody
    In the left hand, harmonize in fourths and fifths
    Create pedal points with your feet

Template 3:  Right hand eighth notes outlining the chords
             Left hand whole note tonic for each measure
             Pedal is in augmentation of the main melody

You can create templates by listening to and looking at scores of professional organists. This is a helpful way to start. If you like a particular recording, listen to it, find a score if possible, and see what is happening musically, then try to imitate that template. Mix and match as many as you can discover. Examine the choices they make, and create your own templates. Think of templates as a formula to help a beginner improvise full pieces. As you progress in the number of pieces you listen to, the level of understanding music theory, your fluency on your instrument, and music you can recreate, you will eventually become more advanced at creating your own music.

## Additional Thoughts

Imagine a piece of music that is 16 bars long. These 16 bars are then repeated exactly the same way seven times in a row. I think it is safe to say that this made-up piece is not very good. Now imagine a hymn 16 bars long that is repeated seven times in a row. Imagine that the composition of the hymn is just a framework, intended to not be complete, and that it's your job to improvise the music. To help tell the story of the hymn and reflect the text of each verse, consider the following options:

| | |
|---|---|
| Change orchestration | Switch parts: melody in the bass |
| Modify harmony | Alter the tempo |
| Compose countermelodies | Shifting dynamics |
| Embroider passing tones in the melody | Modulate to a new key |
| Incorporate pedal points | Insert interludes |

## Timing Exercises (Using Chord Progressions)

With regards to improvising during a Mass, William Picher, music director for the Basilica of the National Shrine of Mary, Queen of the Universe says, "I tell people it's kind of like playing for silent movies. You follow the action. If you need a little bit more time, you stretch out your playing." How does one know how long an improvised section should last?—be present in the moment and observe the action of the clergy and the congregation. For example, the gathering hymn, one should usually wait until the priests are at their seats before finishing the music. During offertory, there is a blessing of the bread and the wine, they wash their hands, then they incense, and finally go back and stand at the altar. During communion, it is important to watch the congregation line to receive communion and anticipate when the last person will receive the body and blood of Christ. Once that happens, the priests bring the Eucharist back to the tabernacle and shut the doors to the tabernacle. As everyone is seated, then taper off the music.

Here is a fun exercise to help develop your timing skills. Try this:

*Liturgical Improvisation* 167

*Level One:*

- Improvise by outlining the chords of a simple chord progression such as: I-IV-V-I.
- Have another person in the room walk a path from one point to another point in the room.
- Make sure you know the starting point, exact path, and end point of the walking student.
- As you repeat your chord progression, the goal is to end on the root chord as the person walking reaches the end point.

*Level Two:*

- Improvise music using more complicated chord progressions such as:

  a.) iii-vi-ii-V-I
  b.) vi-IV-V-I-V-iii-IV-V-I
  c.) I-iii-IV-V-vi-ii-V-I64-V7-I
  d.) i-bVII-bVI-V

- Explore different styles that represent music for gathering, offertory, or communion.
- Have another person in the room walk a path from one point to another point in the room.
- This time, make sure you only know the end point of the walking student.
- As you repeat your chord progression, the goal is to end on the root chord as the walking student reaches the end point.

*Level Three:*

Improvise musical forms that do not create an expectation of symmetry—a musical form that is less linear and more circular. More circular meaning not metered, no symmetric phrasing, no need to finish out a complete phrase, etc . . . so you can stop when you need to stop. For example:

- A chant melody.
- Polyphonic lines in one of the church modes.
- Improvise only using two chords: for example, F7 and Eb7.

**List of Hymns**

This is by no means a comprehensive list of required pieces. Additionally, the type of hymns, of course, depends on the type of associated denomination. However, this can be a good starting point for beginners to learn. Here is a list in alphabetical order:

1. "Amazing Grace"
2. "Crown Him With Many Crowns"
3. "Hail Holy Queen"
4. "Here I Am, Lord"
5. "I Am the Bread of Life"
6. "Immaculate Mary"
7. "Now Thank We All Our God"
8. "On Eagle's Wings"
9. "One Bread, One Body"
10. "Praise God from Whom All Blessings Flow"

168   *Liturgical Improvisation*

### *Contemporary Christian Music*

When listening to contemporary Christian music, it is easy to hear how much it was influenced by gospel, pop, rock, and folk music. As such, the sheet music used while playing this art form, especially for rhythm section players, is in the form of a lead sheet.

*Reading a Lead Sheet*

A lead sheet is a short-hand form of music notation that features the critical information a musician needs to know to adequately perform the music. Notation elements on a lead sheet include chord symbols, key, time signature, melody (but not always), lyrics, slash notation instead of normal notation, etc. See example:

*How to Determine What to Play*

When contemporary musicians look at a lead sheet, how do they know what to play? There are a myriad of options and choices a musician can take when applying the intention to invention process. It would be impossible to list all of the options available to a musician when reading this type of music; however, here are some options a beginner can use to jump-start their training.

*Lead Sheet Options*

Assuming the musician understands the basic theory behind chord symbols, and other musical elements, how then does a musician transform a lead sheet into a pleasing musical sound?

1. Enhance the singing of the hymn.
2. Consider tempo.
3. Understand the meaning of the words.
4. Know the difference between a verse and chorus section.
5. Listen and respond appropriately to your musical environment.
6. Appreciate the importance of not playing.
7. Be a composer, arranger, and orchestrator.
8. Use your imagination.

ENHANCE THE SINGING OF THE HYMN

Any musical choice you make should enhance the singing of the hymn and not interfere or detract from it. Study the piece thoroughly, and as you practice, always ask yourself if what you are doing is serving the music/lyrics or yourself. In this type of music, there will be opportunities to shine through improvised solos, but the bulk of this playing should be supportive.

CONSIDER TEMPO

Tempo is also an important factor to consider, since most of this music is sung. Yes, there are fast tempo songs in this style, but singers will always need time to take breaths and ensure the lyrics are understood by the congregation.

UNDERSTAND THE MEANING OF THE WORDS

The reality is that contemporary Christian musicians are deeply connected to the Word and keep the text in mind as they play. Therefore, it is vital that a novice player study the lyrics, make a personal connection to the lyrics, and allow the text to inform one's musical choices.

KNOW THE DIFFERENCE BETWEEN A VERSE AND CHORUS SECTION

As stated in the previous chapter, there are two main parts of a song—a verse and a chorus. To summarize, verses, in general, are more narrative, musically subtle, more conversational, more rhythmic. Generally speaking, choruses are bigger musical moments involving fewer words that are lyrical with more extended value notes. Knowing that difference both musically and with the text between the two sections will drive your musical choices.

LISTEN AND RESPOND APPROPRIATELY TO YOUR MUSICAL ENVIRONMENT

If you've never performed in a church with contemporary Christian music, let me tell you that no matter how much you practice or rehearse, there will inevitably be something that was not planned.

170   *Liturgical Improvisation*

In these moments, it is critical to listen and respond to your environment. A great example of this: Long ago the worship leader at rehearsal decided that at the end of the arrangement, we will perform the chorus twice before playing the outro. Fast-forward to the worship service, the leader felt in the moment to repeat the chorus three more times before going to the outro. In these unplanned moments, the best thing to do is to go with it and allow the moment to dictate the arrangement.

APPRECIATE THE IMPORTANCE OF NOT PLAYING

As previously stated in this book, whether you are a soloist or an accompanying musician, you do not have to play all of the time. In contemporary Christian worship music, your choices should never be about filling space, rather about supporting the lyrics. Sometimes, stopping altogether and allowing the worship leader to sing a capella can be a very powerful moment for the congregation.

BE A COMPOSER, ARRANGER, AND ORCHESTRATOR

Earlier in this book, I suggested that an improviser be part-composer. I stated that an improviser's thought process needs to mirror that of a composer in terms of translating an idea into a reality by developing a broader perspective on the piece's compositional construction. A lead sheet should be looked at as a guide to help the musicians compose, arrange, and orchestrate. In broad terms, think of composing as creating notes, arranging as deciding the direction of the piece, and orchestration as deciding who plays what. There are endless possibilities. As a beginner, contemplate choosing to

- be more rhythmic,
- be more chordal,
- change octaves,
- create an ostinato,
- rest in some sections,
- change the rhythm based on whether you are in the chorus or in a verse,
- alter the harmony (add chord substitutions),
- change the orchestration: if piano played on the first verse, then have the guitar replace the piano on the second verse, and
- aim for the dominant (if modulation occurs.) A great way to connect two key areas is to slowly introduce or take away accidentals.

USE YOUR IMAGINATION

When improvisers place themselves in a situation outside of their comfort zone, they have two choices: Fight or flee. "Flee" could involve the improviser riddled with apprehension in the moment and thus not play pleasing notes, or maybe not play any notes at all. Whereas "fight" is when an improviser chooses to accept the situation and make it work. When improvisers decide to fight, they are accepting their surroundings and making the best of the situation. In my case, the time between verses was an opportunity to listen to my surroundings and come up with a response. Calling back an earlier story about my first time improvising something other than jazz, (see preface): By listening to my surroundings, I heard the harmonic structure, the hymn style, etc. Using those elements, I imagined what a descant would sound like. I imagined that a descant must be something different than the melody; otherwise, the organist would have asked me to play the melody and not a descant. I also imagined a fanfare-like line—since the name of the hymn was "Crown Him with Many Crowns," and kings typically are associated with fanfares. I thought that fanfares had a lot of arpeggiated patterns with either repeated sixteenth notes or triplets. I trusted the right notes would come out, and if they didn't, I wouldn't let that stop me from playing out. Whatever hymn you are playing, in whatever style, it is important to look for clues in the music so your imagination can lead your musical choices.

Example of options:

Example of options:

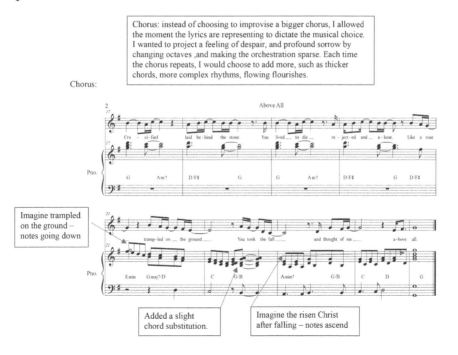

**List of Contemporary Christian Songs**

Here are a few tunes a beginning contemporary Christian artist should study. This is by no means a comprehensive list of required pieces. Additionally, the type of hymns, of course, depends on the type of associated denomination. However, this can be a good starting point for beginners to learn. Here is the list in alphabetical order:

1. "10000 Reasons"
2. "Above All"
3. "Awesome God"
4. "Be Thou My Vision"
5. "Come Thou Fount"
6. "Here I Am to Worship"
7. "In Christ Alone"
8. "It Is Well with My Soul"
9. "Mighty to Save"
10. "Worthy Is the Lamb"

*Essential Elements Applied to Traditional and Contemporary Christian Music*

**1. Trust**

Trust that there are simple, yet effective, ways to improvise in a traditional liturgical setting. Have faith in the process of applying your thought process and musical skills to serve the needs of the religious service. I write about trust many times throughout this book. I do this because trust is the single most crucial aspect of creating with a group of people. An improviser will inevitably develop trust among others. A group of artists who create alongside one another is similar to an athletic team. While there may be star players, even the all-stars need supportive players all working together, trusting one another to do what is necessary to win the game.

**2. Ability to Listen**

Listen and be present in the moment. Be aware of what the clergy are doing at the altar as well as the spontaneous choices a worship leader could make throughout a service.

**3. Synergy**

Artists desire to interact with an audience, tell stories, work with others, and be a part of something bigger than themselves. The effect improvisation has on this sort of collective aspiration opens the door to a venerable state. This state of mind allows a conduit for the creation of art to flow in the moment. Artists engaging in improvisation are mindful enough to understand the goal of the piece and their role in it. They develop a willingness to sacrifice their needs for the sake of the overarching storytelling experience. Improvisation teaches musicians to understand when to fuse into the ensemble and when to stand outside of it.

**4. Micromanagement and Macromanagement**

To macromanage the improvised music, one must be in a constant state of openness, thinking on a broad scope. Hence, improvisers know where to begin, where they are, and where they want to go. This concept is an essential factor to successful improvisation. Be present in the moment, attentive of what is happening and where the piece is going emotionally or artistically.

## 5. Realization

Realize that no matter the style, music is language. Dr. Limb says,

> Language areas lit up, his Broca's area, in the inferior frontal gyrus on the left. He had it also homologous on the right. This is an area thought to be involved in expressive communication. This whole notion that music is a language—maybe there's a neurologic basis to it after all, and we can see it when two musicians are having a musical conversation.

## 6. Stepping into the Deep

Innovation occurs when you step into the deep and try new things. If innovation is the road that leads to a musically enlightened state of consciousness, then improvisation is the vehicle driven on that road. Inspiration to create something new involves insight, problem-solving skills, openness, and risk-taking. Improvisers must draw upon their instincts to resolve problems quickly should they happen in the moment. They must constantly think rapidly about the different perspectives of creating music in the moment. They accept diverse perspectives, detaching from any premeditated expectation. Improvisers who step into the deep and "fight" overcome the fear of failure. Barry Kenny and Martin Gellrich state that mistakes suggest a more pervasive undercurrent that informs all improvisatorial creativity—risk-taking. They go on to state that for improvisers, risk-taking provides a self-induced state of uncertainty where repetition and predictable responses become virtually impossible. I have discovered that the more risks I take, the more mistakes I make. The more mistakes I make, the better my improvisation becomes. The better my improvisation, the more my solos become relaxed and coherent.

## 7. Confidence

Confidence is built very slowly over a long period of time through hard work, experience, knowledge, and preparation. A confident improviser has clear objectives and understands that others can help, encouraging ideas from the team.

## 8. Genuine Study of Craft

If you have a genuine interest in this type of music, I would encourage you to go up to your local church organist or music director or worship leader and ask them questions. Remember that improvisation is a learned craft that takes an enormous amount of time and effort. Have patience and always ask questions!

## 9. Practice

Mr. Earl Carter, my first jazz piano teacher, told me that if I became successful at improv, I would not become the type of artist who succumbs to my own despair, allowing the mistake to define me as a terrible improviser and to stop me from moving forward. Instead, he told me, "You need to rise above your feelings and allow the mistake to push you forward." Why is this? At the time (high school), it wasn't easy to digest, yet the older and more experienced I became, the more I reflected on the truth of what he said. Because an artist who is not making mistakes is probably not trying anything new or taking risks, and thus is not growing into a better artist. Those who embrace mistakes learn from them and use them to propel themselves forward artistically.

## 10. Imagination

I mention earlier in this book, how there is an unlimited supply of musical ideas that live inside the improviser's creative, imaginative mind. It is important for the contemporary and traditional Christian musician to calm the conscious mind in order to access the creative, imaginative mind. Practice letting go of all fears and dissolve the ego. I did not have any prior knowledge on how to improvise a descant or the ability to recognize one visually. However, I did not let that fear take hold. Instead, I imagined the potential sound of a descant. I imagined that a descant must be something different than the melody. Since the tune I was playing was titled "Crown Him with Many Crowns," I imagined the sounds of a room when a king entered and the court bowing before him. I imagined that there would be fanfares played as he processed through the court.

# Final Thoughts

How then do improvisers begin to learn how to fight and not flee? How do they have musical conversations with other improvisers? How do they deactivate the self-censoring part of the brain? To actively choose to "fight" when confronting fear in the moment, my teacher Mr. Carter told me that "you need to first name the fear." Naming the fear has the power to drive it away. When improvisers do not identify the fear, a blurred view occurs, creating more fearful thoughts. Improvisers must ask themselves, *What am I afraid of?* It is ok to be apprehensive about improvisation; just know that there is a solution to every problem.

Having a hard time playing a lot of notes? Play one note, and slowly expand from there. Not sure where to start melodically? Then play the first three notes of a major scale and change up the rhythm. In a creative slump? Then take more time to listen to and study great improvisers or perhaps get inspired by reading a book about your favorite musician. Are you having a hard time with the mechanics of your instrument? Then practice fundamentals.

Apprehensive improvisers must make themselves aware and realize that the only problem they cannot fix is the one they refuse to recognize. The problem with fleeing is it puts improvisation in a special category that only "talented" people can do. While some musicians are more attuned to improvisation than others, this does not mean it is a special skill that a small percentage of musicians can achieve. Anyone can engage in improvisation.

Trust that the exercises that develop improvisational technique have been drilled in practice sessions so that translating an idea into a reality becomes second nature. Novice musicians must not listen to the inner critic that says they cannot do it. Instead, they need to listen to what they want to project and execute what they mentally conceive. They must synergize with the other musicians around them by creating something best for the ensemble, propelling the musical story forward, and micro- and macromanaging their minds to determine what they need to contribute to the conversation. They must step into the deep, forcing themselves into situations where they take on a role never played before or, for novice improvisers, choosing to fight instead of fleeing. They must not be afraid. They must find something that they can latch on to in order to give themselves confidence. At the very least, they can say, "If someone else did it, then it is possible for me to do it." Perhaps the "it" is not the greatest solo ever played, but just a few notes that sound pleasing to the ear. As time goes by, the confidence will grow as skills grow; thus, the act of improvisation will become easier.

The effects of improvisation are endless. Improvisers can respond quicker, go with the flow, and solve problems quickly in the moment. Every new opportunity, every new challenge, is an opportunity to grow and get better. In order to create something brand-new in the moment of performance, one must affirm and then contribute. Saying no or "fleeing" instead of "fighting" ruins any chance of creating something amazing in the moment. Instead, one must resist the urge to give in to the thousand reasons why an idea can't happen and trust that through one's confidence, ability to listen, synergistic view of others, micro and macro processing, realization to step into the deep end of the unknown, and diligent study and practice, one will be able to transmit the intention to an invention, ultimately saying "yes" and discovering what becomes of it.

# Bibliography

Adolphe, Bruce. The Mind's Ear. Oxford University Press. 2013.

Arnold, F.T. The Art of Accompaniment from a Thorough-Bass. Dover Publications. 1965.

Atlas, Alan W. Renaissance Music. W. W. Norton and Company. 1998.

Bailey, Derek. Improvisation Its Nature and Practice in Music. Da Capo Press. 1992.

Brown, Clive. Classical and Romantic Performing Practice. Oxford University Press. 2004.

Carter, Stewart. A Performer's Guide to Seventeenth-Century Music. Indiana University Press. 2012.

Couperin, Francois. L'art de toucher le clavecin. 1716.

Coyle, Daniel. The Culture Code: The Secrets of Highly Successful Groups. Bantam Books. 2018.

Donington, Robert. Baroque Music: Style and Performance: A Handbook. W. W. Norton and Company. 1982.

Donington, Robert. The Interpretation of Early Music. W. W. Norton and Company. 1989.

Duffin, Ross. A Performer's Guide to Medieval Music. Indiana University Press. 2000.

Godt, Irving. Music: A Practical Definition. The Musical Times. Vol. 146. 2005.

Green, Barry. The Mastery of Music: Ten Pathways to True Artistry. Broadway Books. 2003.

Hanning, Barbara. Concise History of Western Music. W. W. Norton and Company. 2014.

Kehneman, Daniel. Thinking Fast and Slow. Farrar, Straus and Giroux. 2013.

Kite-Powell, Jeffery. A Performer's Guide to Renaissance Music. Indiana University Press. 2007.

LaRue, Jan. Guidelines for Style Analysis. Harmonie Park Press. 2011.

Lecture: Charles Limb, Your Brain on Improv. November 5, 2010. https://www.youtube.com/watch?v=BomNG5N_E_0

Lecture: Robert Levin. Experience, Discipline, Fantasy: Improvisation in Classical Music and Jazz. May 24, 2001. https://www.youtube.com/watch?v=ikbJkRX2SGQ

Michalko, Michael. Creative Thinkering. New World Library. 2011.

Palisca, Claude V. Baroque Music. Prentice Hall. 1991.

Parncutt, Richard and McPherson, Gary. The Science and Psychology of Music Performance: Creative Strategies for Teaching and Learning. Oxford University Press. 2002.

Quantz, Johann Joachim. On Playing the Flute. 2nd ed. Northeastern University Press. 2001.

Randel, Don. The New Harvard Dictionary of Music. Belknap Harvard Press. 1986.

Smith, Anne. The Performance of 16th Century Music: Learning from the Theorists. Oxford University Press. 2011.

Stolba, K. Marie. The Development of Western Music A History. Wm C. Brown. 1994.

Stowell, Robin. Violin Technique and Performance Practice in the Late Eighteenth and Early Nineteenth Centuries. Cambridge University Press. 1985.

Tartini, Giuseppe. Treatise on the Ornaments of Music. 1771. Reprinted Carl Fischer. 1956. Virgiliano, Aurelio. Il Dolcimelo. c1600.

Werner, Kenny. Effortless Mastery. Jamey Aebersold Jazz. 1996

Interview with Bill Picher and Peter Latona.

# Index

Note: numbers in *italics* indicate musical score.

Adolphe, Bruce 79
Advent, season of 159
aesthetic: goal of 70; improvisation/improvising compelling notes and 68, 70–77
Aesthetic Exercise 73–77
aleatoric music and free improvisation terminology 113
allegro 32, 45
*Allegro fur das Pianoforte K* (Mozart) 120
andante 32
angry, music expression of 75–76
*application* x, xi, 1, 80, 142–143
applications of intention 10, 80
appoggiatura 46–47, 51
Atlas, Allan W. 111

Bach, J. S. 112, 123
Bailey, Derek 113
Baroque music and terminology 112
blues: secret hidden harmonic melody for 89–90; seven/three resolution and 88–89
blues progression 88; twelve-bar xi
blues scale 83, 85, 86–88; example *87*; recap 92
blues solo, flawed: example *87*
Brown, Clifford 70, 99, 100, 107, 110

cadence, authentic 120–121
cadencing, idea of 118
cadential points 45, 97–98; avoiding tonic as 98 (exercise), 100, 107
cadenza 35, 65; classical period 110; improvised 112; improvising 138; introduction to 112; orchestral 112
Cadenza Exercise 136–139
Carter, Earl 67, 70, 73, 78, 141–142, 173
cartoon music exercise 143
Chance Music Exercises 140

changing harmony within a piece 33
changing rhythm 49; exercise 136
chant 110–111, 117–119
chord changes 66; following 103
chord progressions 95, 166; exercise 61; harmonic 112
chords: connecting one chord to the next, problem and solution 105–106; ii (Dorian) chord 89, 91; dominant 88, 91; dominant seventh chord 84; major seventh 83; minor seventh 83–84; tonic 67, 121; V chord 86, 92; V7 chord 77, 88, 91
chord-scale relationship 72, 73
chord symbols 81, 82–85
chord tones 49; connecting 48; creating resolution between 70; exercise 58, 97–98
Christian (Catholic) liturgical year 158
Christian music, traditional 110; *see also* hymns; liturgical improvisation
Christian songs, contemporary, list of 172
Christmas 159
Christmas carols: "Christmas Song" 42; "Greensleeves" 40; "Hark the Herald" 40; "O Holy Night" 41; "Silent Night" 40
Christmas songs 159; "White Christmas" 42
Christ the King Sunday 159
classical genres, improvisation exercises 117–151; *see also* improvisation exercises
classical language for the jazz improviser 110–116; aleatoric music and free improvisation terminology 113; Baroque music terminology 112; cadenzas, variations, and prologue music terminology 112–113; essential elements for understanding classical language 114–116; Medieval music terminology 110–111; Renaissance music terminology 111–112

*Index* 179

Classical period music: chamber music 78; concerto 35; octatonic scales in 89

classical musicians, jazz improvisation for 81, 91, 95–109; avoiding roadblocks 102–106; beginning to cross over 95–100; essential elements applied when crossing over 106–107; parameters to follow 100; select jazz recordings 107–109; transcribing experts 101–102

constructing a solo 57–68; describing harmonic elements of good solos 59–64; essential elements applied when creating a compelling solo 66–68; essential elements in creating a compelling solo 77–80; exploring melody 57–59; knowing that imagination is limited by technique 65–66; internalizing nuance 65; understanding form of 64–65; *see also* embroidering a solo

Couperin, Francois 112, 123

creative freedom, in improv comedy 145

creative inspiration 6

creative mind, activating 44; with Christian music 174

creative process 2–3, 8; listening as critical part of 73–74, 78; staying focused 144

creative slump, getting out of xii, 68, 76–77, 175

cultivating creativity 69–80; aesthetic as critical component of 70, 73–77; creative slump, getting out of 76–77; essential elements in creating a compelling solo 77–80; groove and 69; inventiveness and 69, 70–72

Davis, Miles 101–102, 107; "Freddie Freeloader" 65; Herbie Hancock playing with 92; Imagine exercise 107; "So What" transcription exercise 101

Debussy 92

depression *see* sadness

Dorian chord 84, 85, 89

Dorian example, improvised chant using 117

Dorian mode 117

Dorian scale 84, 91

Dorian sound 89

double neighbor tones 47

double, in melody 48

Embroider Exercise 50–51

embroidering a solo 44–56; appoggiatura 46–47; changing rhythm 49; chord tones 49; doubles 48; Embroider Exercise 50–51; escape tone 48; essential elements 54–56; filling space 48; glissando 47; mordent 46; neighbor tones 47–48; nonchord tones 49; passing tone 48; sample melodies to embroider 51–54; trill 44–45; turn 45–46; what to play 44–54

escape tone 48

essential elements 1–9; ability to listen 2; bottom line 5 (box); confidence 4; genuine study of the craft 4; imagination 5; micromanagement and macromanagement 2–3; practice 4–5; realization 3; stepping into the deep 3–4; synergy 2; trust 2

essential elements applied to classical improvisation 141–143

essential elements applied to traditional and contemporary Christian music 172–174

essential elements applied when constructing a solo 66–68

essential elements applied when creating a compelling solo 77–80

essential elements applied when crossing over 106–107

essential elements applied when learning the jazz language 92–94

essential elements applied to embroidering the original line 54–56

essential elements for developing an improvisatorial mindset 34–36

essential elements for improv comedic musician 156–157

essential elements for intention 20–21

essential elements for understanding classical language 114–116

filling space 48, 170

Form Exercise 119–122

Free Improvisation Exercise 141–143

fugue 112

Fugue Exercise #2 133–135

Fugue-ish Exercise #1 131–133, 135

Gillespie, Dizzy 35

glissando 47

Godt, Irving 13

groove 72–73; as form of negotiation 69–70

Hancock, Herbie 92

Handel, G. F. 123; "Ode for the Birthday of Queen Anne" (list) 41

Hanning, Barbara 112

happy, music expression of 75–76

hard bop 70

Harmony Exercise 126–137

180   *Index*

hymns: Catholic mass and 158; "Crown Him With Many Crowns" 171; enhancing singing of 169; introductions 159, 162–167; list of 167–171; offertory 161

IAI (Imitate. Assimilate. Innovate) method viii–ix
improv comedy language, improvising music within 145–149
improv comedic musician, improvision for 150–157; essential elements for 156–157; improvising lyrics 150–157
improv comedic song, construction of 149
improvisational mindset, establishing 22–36; essential elements for 34–36; group mind exercises 26–34; imagination etudes 22–26
improvisation exercises 117–151; Cadenza Exercise 136–139; Chance Music Exercises 140; Form Exercise 119–122; Free Improvisation Exercise 141–143; Fugue Exercise #2 133–135; Fugue-ish Exercise I 131–133; Harmony Exercise 126–137; Melodic Exercises 124–126; Multiple Genre Exercises: Silent Film 143–144; Monophonic Exercise 117–118; Polyphonic Exercises 118–119; Prologue Music Exercise 140; Style Exercises 122–124; Variations Exercise 139–140
improvisation, jazz *see* jazz improvisation
improvisation, ten effects of 6 (box), 6–9; Change Management 7 Creative Inspiration 6; Collaboration 8; Enhanced Note Reading 7; Failure 8; Global View 6; Listening Intensifies 7; Possible Impossible Idea 7; Shifting Mindsets 8; Sunk Cost Fallacy 8
improviser as part-composer 42
improviser as part-listener 43
improviser as part-performer 43
improvising between notes 44–56; *see also* see embroidering a solo
improvising for religious (Christian) music *see* liturgical improvisation
improvising lyrics for improv comedy songs 150–157
improvising music within improv comedy 145–149
intention xi; asking questions 15–20; countdown breaths 14–15; essential elements for 20–21; introduction to 10–21; fundamental elements to use 14 (box); mentally conceiving an idea 11–14

invention xii; introduction to 37–43; list of 100; songs to use with conversation exercise 39–42; musical conversation exercise 37–43
inventiveness 70–72; as freedom 69

James, Harry 117
jazz improviser, classical language for 110–116; *see also* classical language for the jazz improvisor 110–116
jazz improvisation for classical musicians 81, 91, 95–109; *see also* classical musicians, jazz improvisation for

LaRue, Jan: *Guidelines for Style Analysis* 14
Latona, Peter 159
legato 17, 32, 100
Levin, Robert 112, 136
Limb, Charles 8–9, 173
liturgical improvisation 150–174; Catholic Mass and music 158–160; contemporary Christian music 168–171; contemporary Christian songs, list of essential works to study 172; essential elements 172–174; hymns 162–167; hymns, list of essential works to study 167; liturgical improvisation strategies 160–166; ostinado options for 160–161, 164
liturgical year 159

marcato 17
McFerrin, Bobby 79
Medieval music terminology 110–111
Melodic Exercises 124–126
Monophonic Exercise 117–118
monophony 110
mordent 45, 46, 51
Movie Music Exercise 144
Mozart, Wolfgang Amadeus 112; *Allegro fur das Pianoforte K* 120; "Queen of the Night Aria" (list) 41
Multiple Genre Exercises: Silent Film 143–144
*Music Man, The* xi

neighbor tones 47–48
nonchord tones 49, 83, 104

organum 110–111
ostinado 160–161, 164; definition of 160

Palisca, Claude V. 113
Parker, Charlie 83, 100
passing tone 48; chromatic (box) 25, 86, 91; nonchord tones as 104; tonic used as 100

pentatonic scale 85; Blues scale as version of 86, 91
Peterson, Oscar 100, 107
Picher, Wiliam 166
Polyphonic Exercises 118–119
polyphony 110–111
Prologue Music Exercise 140

Quantz, Johann Joachim: *On Playing the Flute* 114

Ravel, Claude 92
Renaissance music and terminology 111–112
roadblocks, identifying and avoiding x, 102–106
Rollins, Sonny 70
rounded binary 119–120

sadness, musical expression of 25, 75–76, 158
sample melodies to embroider 51–54
silent film exercise 143–144
silent movies, playing musical accompaniment for 166
simple binary 119
solo *see* constructing a solo; embroidering a solo

staccato 17, 26, 32
Stolba, K. Marie 111
Style Exercises 122–124

Tartini, Giuseppe: *Treatise on the Ornaments of Music* 123
Television Music Exercise 143
ten effects of improvisation 6 (box), 6–9
ten essential elements of improvisers xi, 1 (box); *see also* essential elements. . .
Terry, Clark viii, x
trills 26, 44–45
turn (melodic) 45–46

variation: harmonic variation exercise 139; melodic 124; rhythmic 49, 126; theme and 121
variations, introduction to 112–113
Variations Exercise 139–140
Virgiliano, Aurelio: *Il Dolcimelo* 111, 114, 123

Werner, Kenny 106; *Effortless Mastery* 5, 79
whole-tone scale 92

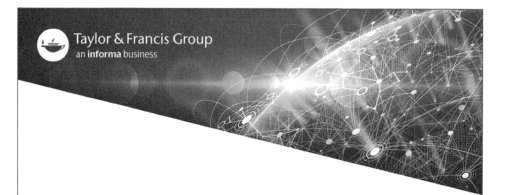

# Taylor & Francis eBooks

www.taylorfrancis.com

A single destination for eBooks from Taylor & Francis with increased functionality and an improved user experience to meet the needs of our customers.

90,000+ eBooks of award-winning academic content in Humanities, Social Science, Science, Technology, Engineering, and Medical written by a global network of editors and authors.

## TAYLOR & FRANCIS EBOOKS OFFERS:

- A streamlined experience for our library customers
- A single point of discovery for all of our eBook content
- Improved search and discovery of content at both book and chapter level

## REQUEST A FREE TRIAL
support@taylorfrancis.com